Communicative Competence:
A Functional-Pragmatic
Approach to Language Therapy

by Charlann S. Simon, M.A. (C.C.C.)
Speech-Language Pathologist

Revised Edition

**Communication
Skill Builders, Inc.** ✱®
3130 N. Dodge Blvd./P.O. Box 42050
Tucson, Arizona 85733

Copyright © 1979, 1981 by

**Communication
Skill Builders, Inc.** ®
3130 N. Dodge Blvd./P.O. Box 42050
Tucson, Arizona 85733
(602) 327-6021

ISBN 0-88450-736-X
Catalog No. 3103

Author's Conceptual View
of Communicative Competence

After a child learns to code his world symbolically with words, he begins to combine them. Initially these are two- to four-word combinations of meaningful words that map the child's communicative intent. Next, structural words are added as the child's language incorporates the grammar of his language community. By the time a child is seven, or perhaps even younger, he begins acquiring socio-centric (as contrasted to his earlier ego-centric) communication skills, in which the informational needs of the listener are considered prior to message formulation. There is a realization, though probably unconscious, that to be effective, a message must be listener-oriented, coherent, fluent and composed of adult grammar. In addition, it becomes apparent that language must service a variety of contexts and purposes and that the demands for specificity and complexity vary according to these contexts and purposes.

If a student shows limited use of the structural code or its functional-pragmatic purposes, he needs to engage in "awareness therapy" which analyzes his communicative assets and deficiencies. As a student becomes more aware of his rights and responsibilities as a speaker, his communication skills will better serve him in his social, educational and occupational experiences.

About the Author

CHARLANN S. SIMON has a B.S. from Northwestern University (1961), an M.A. from the University of Kentucky (1969), and 35 hours of additional graduate study. Her professional positions have included teacher, speech–language clinician in private practice, researcher (Title III, Region IVb project), and language consultant to Clark County Schools (Kentucky). Her present professional positions are speech–language clinician and consultant to the Devereux Foundation (Scottsdale, Arizona), adjunct assistant professor at Arizona State University (Tempe, Arizona), and consultant to the Arizona Department of Education (Phoenix). Her articles have been published in the *Journal of Speech and Hearing Disorders; Kentucky English Bulletin; Language, Speech and Hearing Services in Schools;* and *Thinking: A Journal of Philosophy for Children.* She has also conducted mini–seminars and presented papers at American Speech and Hearing Association conventions and has been a visiting consultant to many public school systems within the United States and Canada.

Acknowledgements

The author wishes to acknowledge the editorial contributions of Dr. Sharon Murray, Carl Miller, and Mary Carr of the Children's Speech and Hearing Center in Washington, D.C.; Carolyn Ausberger of Maricopa Speech and Hearing Consultants, Phoenix, Arizona; Connie McCarthy of the Washington School District, Phoenix, Arizona; and Kathy Salcito, Tucson Unified School District, Tucson, Arizona; and the graduate students in my Fall 1978 seminar at Arizona State University. In addition, I want to express appreciation for the understanding shown by my family and publisher during multiple revisions of the manuscript. Finally, I wish to express gratitude to Dr. Eric K. Sander of Cleveland State University, Cleveland, Ohio, who established in me a sense of excitement with the professional literature and a respect for how new knowledge being generated through research can stimulate clinical practices.

The use of the masculine pronoun form throughout the book is for convenience and brevity and is not intended to be preferential or discriminatory.

CONTENTS

LIST OF TABLES

INTRODUCTION

Communicative competence is essential for social, personal, and educational growth. This monograph describes and discusses one approach to language evaluation and therapy that has evolved over a decade of clinical experience and study of theoretical and empirical explorations of language competence versus language incompetence.

To be competent, language must be functional.

> Being appropriate to the situation is not some optional extra in language; it is an essential element in the ability to mean. . . . Our functional picture of the adult linguistic system is of a culturally specific and situationally sensitive range of meaning potential. Language is the ability to mean in the situation types or social contexts that are generated by culture. When we talk about "uses of language" we are concerned with the meaning potential that is associated with particular situation types (Halliday 1978, p. 34).

"Communicative competence" is a term associated with the work of Hymes (1971). It refers to competence in the use of language, or the speaker's ability to use language in ways that are appropriate to the situation. Osser (1969) described two characteristics or elements of communicative competence: (1) the ability to analyze the listener's role characteristics, and (2) the ability to use one's linguistic resources in appropriate communication strategies. The notion of developing a language means to add to its range of social functions (Halliday 1978). An underdeveloped language is one that serves only some functions, but not all functions.

It is the thesis of this monograph that the clinician should develop a comprehensive view of expressive communicative competence that encompasses considerations of both language form and function. Pragmatic considerations such as speaker–listener roles, the context in which the communication takes place, and the effectiveness with which the speaker's communicative intent is expressed to the listener are all part of a functional view of language; the focus is on how well communication attempts "work" for an individual. "From a functional view, the process of learning one's language is the progressive mastery of a number of basic functions of language and building meaning potential in respect of each" (Halliday 1978, p. 21).

To ensure comprehensive programming, the clinician needs to formulate a conceptual model that describes competent versus incompetent communication behaviors. This conceptual model provides justification for evaluation and programming procedures used by the clinician. It serves as a standard against which an individual's communication behavior is measured, as well as a description of those behaviors that contribute to the listener's impression that the speaker is incompetent. It must be a dynamic model — one that is continuously being refined by new clinical insights and research findings. It should never be a static, blindly accepted model proposed by a test, a program, or another professional.

The author presents in Table 1 an example of a clinician's conceptual model. This model will be defined and discussed in this monograph. Its emphasis is on expressive language. The reader is referred to Wiig and Semel (1976) for an example of a receptive language model and to Lasky and Chapandy (1976) as well as Rees and Shulman (1978) for excellent analyses and discussions of receptive competence.

A clinician's model can be "adaptive" or "synthetic." An example of an adaptive model is Wiig and Semel's (1976) use of Guilford's (1967) Structure of Intellect model for explaining the various demands made upon receptive and expressive language capabilities. The model defined and discussed in this monograph is synthetic. It has been constructed by combining and intertwining various theoretical models and empirical findings. In addition, clinical observations of effective versus ineffective communication styles and behaviors have been incorporated.

Two assumptions are basic to the author's clinical approach:

1. Research and application are not separate spheres. Journals, monographs, and books in speech–language pathology, psychology, education, and other related fields should be regularly perused for information that is relevant to the communication process and therapy (or management of communication problems). A profession remains stimulating when one views one's present knowledge as only the *kernel* of inquiry. New knowledge can (and should) have a significant impact on the clinician's basic philosophical tenets, evaluation procedures, and programming goals.

2. Each clinician must begin evaluation and therapy with a conception of what constitutes proficient communication as opposed to nonproficient communication. This conception (or model) should be dynamic, as opposed to static, because of the constant input from new knowledge about communication that is continuously made available. In other words, each clinician's model should be dynamic because of infusion, adaptation, and refinement resulting from familiarity with the professional literature and from clinical experiences.

Communicative Competence: A Functional–Pragmatic Approach to Language Therapy has been organized into three components:

1. A theoretical monograph, which discusses the author's clinical model or rationale for the procedures suggested to the clinician.

2. A set of stimulus materials that enable the clinician to implement the theoretical model proposed by the author.

3. A manual that offers some specific suggestions to the clinician for using the stimulus materials developed by the author as well as other materials available that can supplement the basic program components presented.

This theoretical monograph is composed of four sections: Section I, Some Thoughts on the Application of Research; Section II, The Conceptual Model of Communicative Competence; Section III, Underlying Premises that Guide Clinician Practices; and Section IV, Examples of Incompetent Communication.

This monograph is dedicated to children in public and private schools who deserve, as part of their educational process, the opportunity of arriving at their "meaning potential" through developing more effective communication skills.

> The processes of becoming educated require that the child's meaning potential should have developed along certain lines in certain types of contexts, especially in relation to the exploration of the environment and of his own part in it. . . . Certain ways of organizing experience through language and of participating and interacting with people and things are necessary to success in school. The child who is not predisposed to this type of verbal exploration in this type of experiential and interpersonal context is not at home in the educational world (Halliday 1978, p. 26).

Although the masculine pronouns (he, his, him) are used to refer to clinical case examples, the author does not intend to imply that only males experience language problems. This is merely a convenient literary device.

TABLE 1

A Clinician's Model of Expressive Communicative Competence

COMPETENT FEATURES			INCOMPETENT FEATURES		
FORM	**FUNCTION**	**STYLE**	**FORM**	**FUNCTION**	**STYLE**
flexible, precise vocabulary	sustains topics of conversation	considers listener's informational needs	limited vocabulary repeated often	wanders from conversational topic	egocentric comments
mastery of syntactic and morphological rules	selected phrasing reflects communicative intent	advance planning of content	syntactic and morphological errors	ineffective illocutionary speech acts	incoherent sequencing of details
complexity and variety of syntax	gives support for a point of view	finds words easily to express thoughts	basic syntactic patterns re-used	opinions stated as fact	word-finding difficulty
mastery of irregular grammatical features	uses elaborated and restricted codes	fluency in expression	difficulty with irregular verbs, plurals, and comparatives	relies upon restricted code	false starts (mazes)
mastery of tense reference and subject/verb agreement	social and cognitive uses of language	intelligible, distinct speech	lacks consistency in tense and number reference	informal, social uses of language	slurred speech consisting of a series of "giant words"
uses clear noun referents	developed heuristic language function	comfortable speech rate	uses ambiguous pronouns	afraid to ask adults questions	rapid, jerky speech rate
uses subordinators to relate ideas	contextual adaptations of language	audible speech	unsystematic combinations of ideas	limited language flexibility	speech volume not adapted to context
	tactful deviousness used			tactless statements	
	modifies and clarifies message upon listener request			restates same information	

SECTION I
Some Thoughts on the Application
of Research

INTRODUCTION

A major difference between an "aide" and a "clinician" is that the latter must assume the responsibility of working from a conceptual model of what constitutes competent versus incompetent (or deviant) communication. A conceptual model provides the underlying purposes for evaluation and programming strategies; it provides the documentation for *why* the clinician engages in one strategy as opposed to another.

We are living in a "data boom," and that means that it is essential to remain abreast of changing trends in the interpretation of communication development and the impediments to that development. New and more persuasive data can shake the roots of one's conceptual model — stimulating, rather than devastating, those roots.

CHANGING TRENDS

Research on language learning and development has been generated from many different theoretical models. Let's look at the changing trends and the shifts in focus over the past twenty years.

With the advent of the theory of generative transformational grammar (Chomsky 1957), the search for grammar became the goal of language research in the 1960s. The dominant theoretical position in these studies was that syntax was systematic and that words were not juxtaposed at random, even in the earliest sentences. To paraphrase Dale (1976):

> Language is a productive system in which novel sentences can be generated. One must only master the set of principles that specify how words can be combined to form sentences. With a finite amount of knowledge, the speaker can understand or produce an unlimited number of sentences. The child achieves a creative ability to produce novel, rule–governed utterances from the beginning of the two–word stage.

Researchers rejected the notion espoused by Skinner (1957) and other behaviorists that the child's language knowledge and resulting performance developed from imitation alone. The errors children made indicated that grammar learning was not acquired by rote memory; the child, it seemed, acquired something of the adult language around him, but then filtered it through his own actively constructing and emerging grammatical system.

The "pivot–open" model (Braine 1963; McNeill 1970; Slobin 1968) was an early attempt to describe the productive but idiosyncratic child system, as well as its errors (or departures from the adult system). This distributional analysis showed a small group of words occurring with great frequency in fixed order relative to a larger group of words in the child's speech. Pivot grammar rules said nothing, however, about the meaningful relations between words and did very little to explain how the child achieves linguistic creativity (or how he goes on to produce increasingly complex, novel sentences) (Bloom 1975).

In the 1970s attention was turned from description to an attempt to explain early sentences. "A search began for the cognitive correlates of meaning in language and the cognitive processes involved in language learning" (Bloom 1975, p. 249). As Beilin (1975) points out, while the cognitive and linguistic systems are sufficiently different to exclude direct mapping or a causal link, "the correlations found between linguistic and cognitive milestones suggest that the two aspects of development are indeed connected intricately" (Bowerman 1978, p. 120). This "interactionist hypothesis" suggests that language and cognition are "in training" together. The author concurs with this position.

Schlesinger (1971) and Bloom (1970) proposed describing sentences not only in terms of their word classes and combinations, but also in terms of the functions that the words served in the sentences. Brown (1973) described 75 percent of these relationships as most commonly occurring in the two–word stage of development. A set of eight descriptive semantic–grammatical rules was generated from the research of Brown, Bloom and Schlesinger which explained the underlying semantic intentions that were coded in the surface forms of a child's early utterances (MacDonald and Blott 1974; MacDonald 1978). Nelson's (1973) research indicated that most children acquire at least fifty words before beginning to put two words together and that these early words describe the child's personal interactions with his environment. That children characteristically talk about the immediate and perceptually evident events in their environment has been observed by other researchers as well, including Bloom (1970) and Brown and Bellugi–Klima (1964).

Piaget (Sigel and Cocking 1977) notes that most significant achievement of sensorimotor development is the realization that the world consists of enduring objects located in a spatial framework upon which the infant and other persons can act. Bloom (1970) and Brown (1973) postulate that the basic relations expressed by child language can be viewed as the linguistic expression of sensorimotor intelligence. They are quick to remind us that there may be inequities, however, between the development of a concept and the ability to express it. Because a child does not express certain relationships, one should not *assume* that he does not have the concept.

It is not surprising that the child's earliest sentences are about agents, the actions they perform, the objects on which they act, and the locations of persons and objects. The child talks about what he experiences. Because of the child's limited vocabulary (or core lexicon), it is necessary to consult the context in which an utterance occurred to fully appreciate or understand its meaning. In other words, this small vocabulary is "milked" by the child; the same small number of words is used over and over again to convey varying intentions. While the *form* of two utterances may be the same, they might serve different *functions*. The observer must focus on the nature of the relationship between the two words. "Baby blanket" contains two nouns, but the nature of the relationship between the two nouns can only be determined by the setting (which is why the complexity of a child's language at this stage of development cannot be estimated by only looking at the words used). Bloom's (1970) classic example focused on the utterance "Mommy sock." In one context it meant "This is Mommy's sock," but in another context it meant "Mommy, put on my sock." (While one cannot guarantee that every adult interpretation of a child's utterance reflects the child's thinking strategies, as contrasted to the adult's thinking strategies, the context certainly aids the adult in making an objective interpretation.) Pivot grammar does not map these functions (nor the communicative intent), only the form; the semantic–grammatical rule explanation is more complete. Most recently, the study of the pragmatic aspects of language development has focused even more closely on the context of utterances and the speaker–listener role expectations involved.

From early interest in the child's acquisition of syntax and the more recent assertions that language acquisition is a matter of the child learning how the language expresses his cognitive impressions of the world, research trends have shifted to studies that relate the development of language to its uses in social context and discourse. A much more comprehensive view of communicative competence has evolved as the result of research that has taken more and more of a cultural perspective. When language is viewed in terms of interactions, then the social system automatically becomes a component and language assumes a critical role in the transmission of culture (Halliday 1978). Evaluation and therapy strategies should reflect the depth and breadth of our profession's understanding of the communication process.

APPLICATION OF RESEARCH IN EVALUATION OF COMMUNICATION SKILLS

We are always searching for better ways to analyze the components of communication competence. Reports of these investigations appear in the professional literature and permit the clinician to refine evaluation practices. New information can be classified into at least seven types:

1. *Introduction of New Standardized Tests.* Preliminary findings are presented on the standardization of assessment instruments that the authors have developed (Lee 1970; Carrow 1974). If the instrument appears useful, as well as reliable and valid, the clinician can watch for its publication.

2. *Description of Informal Measures.* Fortunately, we have reached a point in our maturity as a discipline where we do not feel that *all* evaluation must be summarized in numbers, or that an individual child's performance has to be compared to a standardization population. For example, Chappell and Johnson (1976) devised a series of tasks to observe the cognitive functioning of nonverbal children. Nelson–Burgess (1975) developed a receptive language test for bilingual children, and Monsees and Berman (1968) devised a screening test of a summer Headstart program. Leonard *et al* (1978) discussed the value of informal observations of the child's communicative competence, with particular reference to the new research in pragmatics.

3. *Clinician Adaptation of Research Tasks.* The purpose of linguistic research is to investigate the nature of language and language dysfunction. Some of the tasks designed to investigate these behaviors can be used informally by clinicians. For example, when a child performs very poorly on the *Test for Auditory Comprehension of Language* (Carrow 1973), the author uses Bellugi–Klima's (1971) comprehension tasks. The child is used to act out various constructions with toys (e.g., "Show me, 'The boy is chasing the girl.' "). In assessing a child's referential skills, the author adapted the research task described by Glucksberg and Krause (1967). The clinician and child have identical sets of objects. The clinician places a screen between the child and himself and asks the child to arrange the objects in some kind of relationship to each other and then to provide the clinician with directions for reproducing the same relationship among the objects. If the child says "Put this thing here," he obviously is not communicating with his listener's needs in mind!

4. *New Reliability and Validity of Published Tests.* Assessment instruments should not be viewed as products of intuitive wisdom that are not to be questioned or improved upon. The clinician should keep abreast of critical research and observations on published tests. For example, the *Illinois Test of Psycholinguistic Abilities* (Kirk, McCarthy and Kirk 1968) now has its own listing in the *Educational Index* because so many studies have been published that were designed to investigate the reliability and validity of the conceptual model, scoring procedures, and content of the subtests. Only a few examples of these will be shared here. Cronkhite and Penner (1975) suggested that the use of factor analysis profiles would be more meaningful than the use of subtest profiles. Duncan and Baskervill (1977) and Arnold and Reed (1976) commented on the differences in performance on the Grammatic Closure subtest between Black and Caucasian school children as well as the implications for the analysis of findings and subsequent programming. Two of the ITPA authors, Kirk and Kirk (1978), responded to many of the criticisms of the ITPA by restating its purposes and limitations. There are many other tests that are used by

9

clinicians frequently enough that their limitations are perceived or questions arise about the appropriateness of the standardization population for a particular child or region. Kresheck and Nicolosi (1973) compared performances of Black and Caucasian children on the *Peabody Picture Vocabulary Test* (PPVT) (Dunn 1965), and in 1972 they investigated the variability in test scores on Form A and Form B of this widely used test. While the first research project indicated a limited clinical value of the PPVT with "low–middle class" Black children, the other project showed that Form B of the PPVT is considerably more difficult than Form A. This means that if the clinician administers Form A initially, it should also be used for comparative data. Seigel and Broen (1976) have provided some very complete guidelines for evaluating the reliability and validity of assessment procedures.

5. *Usefulness of a Test from a Related Academic Discipline.* Wiig and Semel (1976) have analyzed the usefulness of many tests from psychology, education, and other related fields. They have organized this information on assessment in terms of subtests that tap specific auditory processing, cognitive processing, and expressive language skills. Each test and subtest is organized in terms of the behavior observed, described, and referenced with publisher information. In addition, Ratusnik and Koenigsknecht (1976) discussed the 1972 revision of the *Columbia Mental Maturity Scale* (Burgemeister, Blum and Lorge 1972). They found it relatively free of racial bias and suitable for multicultural clinical use. Rees and Shulman (1978) comment that current "language comprehension tests" do not investigate presupposition, inference, and illocutionary acts. They recommended subtests of instruments designed for intelligence and reading skill evaluation and tests for adult aphasia as sources of more complex comprehension items that require linguistic integration and inference.

6. *Language Sampling Contexts and Techniques.* The purpose of a language sample is to collect a representative, spontaneous example of an individual's communicative competence. This means that a *variety* of real or simulated contexts is ideal because we want to observe how well the individual flexibly *uses* language. Longhurst and Grubb (1974) have discussed how context affects one's impressions about the maturity and effectiveness of a child's language, and Longhurst and Schrandt (1973) investigated various techniques of sample analysis. Lee (1974) provides an informative chapter on eliciting responses from a child that would permit him to display a variety of structures and encourage his greatest complexity of construction. Muma (1972) provides some comprehensive considerations on sampling and how informal and formal correlate measures should be used as supplementary data on the child's communication performance. Prutting, Gallagher and Mulac (1975) attend to a comparison of a child's spontaneous language with a standardized expressive test.

7. *Clinician Effects on the Child's Performance.* Communication does not occur in a vacuum; it is the result of interaction. The variables within the context of that interaction can affect the quality and quantity of the content. For example, Berry and Erickson (1973) found that the rate of examiner speech had a significant effect upon test performance. The examiner should adopt a deliberate rate of speech when administering test items. Olswang and Carpenter (1978) investigated elicitor versus maternal effects on the language obtained during sampling procedures. The results of the study indicated that "the clinician, as an unfamiliar person to the child, should feel relatively confident in his or her ability to elicit as qualitatively good a language sample from a young child as the child's mother" (p. 85) when using Lee's (1974) guidelines. The children in the Olswang and Carpenter study were below six years of age and had MLUs (mean length of utterances) of between one to two morphemes. "Perhaps elicitor effects would appear in children with better developed grammatical or semantic abilities" (p. 85). Labov (1970) would strongly agree with this supposition as it relates to language sampling of language–different children. He emphasizes that the manner in which an adult interacts with a child has significant effects on the quality of his output. He offers as an example a Caucasian interviewer sitting at a table and saying to a Black student "Tell me everything

you can about this (toy on the table)," versus a Black interviewer from the neighborhood who brings a sack of potato chips, sits on the floor, creates a party atmosphere, speaks in the child's vernacular, and encourages a friend of the child being interviewed to also participate.

The author has not attempted to review all of the literature that has pertinent considerations for the clinician's evaluation procedures. The above discussion merely taps the surface. The purpose of this section has been to enumerate some of the ways in which the clinician can use data appearing in journal articles, books, and monographs to refine current knowledge about assessment.

APPLICATION OF RESEARCH IN PROGRAMMING — AN EXAMPLE

Prior to the abundance of research that focused on the semantic intention underlying syntax, language programs based on structural expansion were developed. The concept of linear stringing of structural units (is, is red, ball is red, the ball is red) was combined with programmed conditioning of verbal behavior (Gray and Ryan 1973). "Thousands of children were being taught to talk" (Ryan 1978). Were they, however, taught to "mean"? Gray and Ryan's (1973) programmed conditioning format is contrary to the evidence we now have about the way in which children naturally expand utterances. The child begins with the most meaningful words and then adds functors (or the less meaningful, grammatically necessary words). From this semantic orientation, it could be predicted that a child would reach the sentence, "The ball is red," by the following process: ball, red ball, ball is red, the ball is red.

MacDonald and Blott (1974) and MacDonald (1978), making use of the research of Brown (1973), Bloom (1970), and Schlesinger (1971), developed the Environmental Language Intervention Strategy (see Appendix 2). It is composed of eight semantic-grammatic rules and uses the child's immediate environmental context to build a lexicon and then to formulate two-word utterances. In other words, the focus is on the child talking about his "here and now" world.

When faced with a programming decision for a five-year-old nearly nonverbal child who has been described by a psychiatrist as "autistic-like," should the clinician choose the Gray and Ryan (1973) approach or the approach proposed by MacDonald and Blott (1974)? Since data have overwhelmingly demonstrated that children beginning to communicate do not string forms together like a robot, but talk about meaningful relationships in their environment, the MacDonald and Blott model (or other semantically-based models) is more congruent with our current advances in research. (A case study reported by Fygetakis and Ingram, 1972, demonstrates an attempt to reconcile the semantically-based model of language development with the programmed conditioning format.) By remaining actively in touch with more comprehensive explanations of the communication process, the clinician is in a position to reject one approach (that might be lying on the clinic shelf just waiting to have a child plugged into it!) and to insist upon a more appropriate approach. The clinician is able to justify preferred methodology in view of the most current empirical and theoretical contributions to the field of communication.

Continuing with an example of research application, let us suppose that our hypothetical "autistic-like" clinic child (who was making only minimal affective contact and whose utterances were composed of jargon and whining rather than vocabulary) has progressed to a forty-word intelligible vocabulary and is beginning to comment on his environment through various two-word semantic-grammatical rules. What is the next step? Research indicates that children begin *combining* semantic-grammatical rules within an utterance before they start adding functors and inflections (Brown 1973; Ingram 1972). In other words, it is more likely that a child will express *two* relationships before mapping one relationship in adult syntax. "Boy run" would more likely be expanded to "Boy run here," than "The boy is running." The child relies upon contentives (words that carry meaning), making early expanded sentences telegraphic, or lacking in prepositions, articles, copulas, auxiliaries, inflections (like –ed, –ing, –s), or other functors (Brown 1973). The clinician, therefore, would want to encourage the child to combine an agent/action construction (such as "dog run") with an action/location construction ("run here") to produce a *three*-word construction showing two relationships ("dog run here"). The extra length is typically achieved through the combination of relationships that have already been expressed in individual two-word utterances. Researchers conclude that the shift from two- to three- to four-word sentences reflects a lifting of some kind of constraint — perhaps memory, as opposed to the ability to map new relationships. With the longer utterances the child seems to be showing the memory capacity for combining more semantic-grammatical rules (Brown 1973; Bowerman 1978).

When the child shows an MLU of approximately 3.0, "is" appears as a structural unit (Ingram 1972). Noted by both Brown (1973) and Ingram (1972), "is" first appears as a copular (or linking) verb ("He *is* big"), rather than as an auxiliary verb ("He *is* running"). Ingram additionally recommends that the contracted form ("He's big") should be introduced to the language-deficient child before the uncontracted form ("He *is* big"). Ingram emphasizes that since only 25 percent of children's utterances have obligatory contexts for this structure, programming should not concentrate solely on the child's acquisition of "is" but should continue to stress semantic-grammatical relations, pronouns, and other functors (in addition to "is").

As the clinician developmentally guides the child toward adult grammar, Lee's Complexity Index (1974, see Appendix 3), which was devised to score sentences in terms of deep structure rather than surface length, can be consulted. (While this may not be a perfect tool, it can be modified as new, contradictory research appears.) For our hypothetical case, functors at Level One on Lee's Complexity Index would gradually be added.

One of the language clinician's tasks is to teach sentence structure. The example of research application presented here has focused upon how the clinician can use research evidence to developmentally sequence early structural training. Through this semantically-based procedure, the child becomes increasingly able to express his thoughts, feelings, and perceptions in a manner that can be more completely understood by his language community.

In review, the following suggestions, drawn from empirical data, were offered to the clinician faced with the task of sequencing a language program for a child of age five who relied upon jargon and whining for communication when he entered therapy:

1. Help the child acquire between thirty-five (Holland 1975) and fifty words (Nelson 1973) that describe his personal interactions with the environment. In doing so, a flexible core lexicon is generated from the child's world.

2. Using the guidelines established by MacDonald and Blott (1974) and MacDonald (1978), encourage the child to verbalize about relationships in his environment using the semantic-grammatical rules to formulate two-word utterances.

3. Combine semantic-grammatical rules to produce three- and four-word utterances (Ingram 1972; Brown 1973).

4. At approximately 3.0 MLU, begin to introduce grammatical forms. While these do not carry any meaning, they are part of the adult linguistic system, which is the ultimate competency goal for the child. Begin with the contractible form of the copular verb "is" and subjective pronouns (Ingram 1972).

5. Teach additional grammatical forms developmentally, beginning with those that appear at Complexity Level One on Lee's (1974) Developmental Sentence Scoring Index (Appendix 3).

Maintaining a view of language as "a tool of use," the language-learning child should be exposed to a variety of communication contexts in which he has opportunities to use language for various purposes (Rees 1978; Halliday 1973, 1978).

Sift and Sequence

A "sift and sequence" attitude is recommended to the clinician interested in using research as a reference to updating philosophy and procedures. In the example provided above, pivot grammar (Braine 1963; McNeill 1970) was "sifted" as a philosophical position for describing early two-word combinations in favor of the semantically-based explanations of Schlesinger (1971), Bloom (1970) and Brown (1973), which not only focused on form, but the meaningful relations between and among forms. Likewise, when deciding upon a therapy procedure to develop language, the programmed, linear stringing approach of Gray and Ryan (1973) was "sifted" and the MacDonald and Blott (1974) and MacDonald (1978) approach accepted. The latter permitted and encouraged the child to develop a mini-language that would manipulate the environment, thus providing immediate "pay-offs" from the new linguistic knowledge. In addition, this strategy was in accordance with research findings on normal language development.

Research findings and recommendations by Holland (1975) and Nelson (1973) on the development of an initial lexicon, by Ingram (1972) and Brown (1973) on the introduction of functors, and by Lee (1974) on later developing grammatical structures were "sequenced" so that they could be drawn upon at the appropriate time in programming.

SEQUENCING A CHILD'S NEEDS, CONCEPTUAL MODELS, AND LANGUAGE PROGRAMS

Priorities

As the clinician views the child's "language deficient profile," it is necessary to prioritize his needs. If an eight-year-old child is "sputtering" his perceptions and thoughts in an incoherent manner, reverses word order in questions, and lisps, a decision about what to emphasize has to be made by the clinician. The author suggests that the clinician sequence the child's program in terms of a general-to-specific reference point. For example, within the clinician's model of competent communication, all of these behaviors would need attention, but which behavior most pervasively contributes to the listener's impression that this child is an incompetent communicator? For this eight-year-old, it would be crucial that he first learn to organize his thoughts prior to expression and provide the listener with quality, not quantity, of output. As this behavior is coming under control, emphasis on word order in questions could be introduced. The clinician could continue to build coherent expressive skills along with teaching interrogative syntax. The remediation of the lisp should be considered a refinement. While this behavior might "call attention to itself" in a coherent speaker, it would be insignificant to the listener trying to decipher the communicative intent of a child whose messages are nearly incoherent.

Models and Programs

The clinician should consider sequencing not only research findings, but conceptual models and language programs as well. For example, there might be several language programs or teaching strategies available, prompting the clinician to wonder which one to use. Ask a basic question: "What does the child need at this point in his development to make him a more competent communicator?" You might find that you need to draw from several models or programs simultaneously. The point is — let the child's needs guide the selection of any one component of therapy; it is highly unlikely that a clinician could, *with justification,* arbitrarily take any child through the steps of one program to the exclusion of all other input. No program is that comprehensive nor can any author anticipate the exact sequence of events through which all language–deficient children should pass.

For an example of sequencing conceptual models and language programs, let's return to our five–year–old hypothetical clinic child (described on page 12). The Environmental Language Intervention Strategy (MacDonald and Blott 1974; MacDonald 1978) was initially used to provide the child with functional communication skills at the two-word level. As functors are introduced, a drill approach might be needed because, initially, the insertion of functors seems to be a memory process rather than a linguistic rule that is immediately internalized. The child needs to drill on the obligatory contexts of the particular functor. The clinician could consider a syntactic slot–filler approach (Weiss and Duffy 1974) supplemented with blocks representing words in the construction or a commercial program that provides strong visual support in learning these grammatical forms (Ausberger 1976). Even though functors seem meaningless to the child, they are meaningful to the language system. Keeping in mind that language is defined for the child by its uses (Halliday 1973), the child should be told *why* he has to learn these "little meaningless words." For example, "This little buzz–word (is) *has* to be here. That's the way our language works. We want *your* speech to sound the same as speech in books." A favorite book might be read aloud to illustrate this, with the clinician verbally emphasizing the word "is" and even pointing to it.

After several rudimentary grammatical constructions have reached an 80 to 90 percent criterion level in this type of drill, combine them in a story to be presented within the Interactive Language Development Teaching format (Lee, Koenigsnecht and Mulhern 1974).

Appropriate at various stages of therapy are the child–initiated and clinician–initiated techniques described by Muma (1973), which help the child test his hypothesis of how the language works. Both the Lee, Koenigsnecht and Mulhern (1974) and the Muma (1973) approaches stress dialogue, which begins to establish contextual reasons for using the new structures. The Halliday (1973) model should also be used by the clinician to devise programming segments that allow the child "to practice" using his new linguistic skills to perform a variety of language functions (instrumental, regulatory, interactional/personal, heuristic, imaginative, and informational). This monograph stresses the necessity of keeping the listener's needs in mind when descriptions and instructions are given. *Communicative Competence: A Functional–Pragmatic Language Program* (Simon 1980, available from Communication Skill Builders, Inc.) will help the child focus on refining interpersonal communication skills.

EXPLORING THE VERSATILITY OF RESEARCH FINDINGS AND TEACHING STRATEGIES

The clinician is encouraged to view research findings, theoretical insights, and communication teaching strategies in a creative manner rather than through a tunnel. Let's consider some example of exploring the versatility of information.

Avoiding Categorical Thinking

When reading a research report or a case study, do not process it categorically. For example, if the title of an article is "Creative Thinking Abilities of Cleft Palate Children," or "A Therapeutic Milieu for Establishing and Expanding Communicative Behaviors in Psychotic Children," the data presented are frequently not limited just to those etiological classifications.

Bereiter and Englemann (1966) discuss how "cultural deprivation" (defined by the authors as "a lack of those particular kinds of learning that are important for success in school") affects the disadvantaged pre–school child. One of their major theses is that it is the absence of the "cognitive uses of language" (to explain, describe, instruct, inquire, hypothesize, analyze, compare/contrast, deduce, and test) that contributes significantly to academic failure. Obviously, these insights are not limited to "pre-school children" nor "disadvantaged children." It is a relevant consideration when programming for any child who is having difficulty with "school language."

Manual communication was, for many years, a strategy reserved for the deaf. Obviously, this was the epitome of tunnel vision. Over the past five years there have been numerous reports at conventions (Bennett 1974; Casey 1976) and in the professional literature (Mayberry 1976; Skelly *et al* 1974; Bonvillian and Nelson 1976; Brookner and Murphy 1975) on the use of signing to facilitate communication skills in cases with a variety of etiological labels. What a waste it has been that the versatility of this mode of communication was not explored more thoroughly and publicized earlier.

Versatility of Programs

Regarding language teaching models and commercial programs that can be creatively manipulated to meet clinician needs, three examples from the author's experience are shared.

First, the versatility of the Environmental Language Intervention Strategy (ELIS) was explored (Simon 1976). This strategy was developed by MacDonald and Blott (1974) and MacDonald (1978) to work with mentally retarded children. The author also found it to be an effective technique for teaching core language concepts to autistic children, because it provided a simplified code (two *meaningful* words) with which they could manipulate their environment. Perhaps feedback problems (Yudkovitz and Rottersman 1973) experienced by these children inhibit their ability to "crack the code" at the adult syntax level. Once this "reduced code" (semantic–grammatical rules) was learned, it was expanded (in most of the children) to four- to five-word utterances using somewhat primitive adult syntax. It seemed as if some kinds of constraints prevented a few children from generating totally accurate syntax even after two to three years of therapy. More importantly, however, they developed a *creative* language that permitted them to express their frustrations verbally rather than acting out. The refinements of adult syntax may be yet to come.

Two additional uses of the ELIS (Simon 1976) mentioned were:

1. From consultations with learning disabilities teachers, it was observed that instead of teaching sight words (for reading) within a functional context, they were usually just flashed one at a time ("boy," "dog," "run"). It was suggested that teachers use the eight semantic–grammatical rules to teach these words within a semantic context ("boy run," "dog run") rather than in a visual symbol vacuum. A subsequent study by the author (Simon 1978) indicated a significant improvement in memory of sight words when they were presented within this semantic context.

2. Classroom teachers in readiness classes, as well as special education settings, frequently complain about how poorly children respond to verbal directions. Instead of repeating many times a directive that is embedded in a complex syntactic construction, teachers were encouraged to simplify the verbal direction the second time it is given to include only two to three words. For example,

15

"I want you to color this wagon with your red crayon" can be simplified to "Color wagon red." The ELIS article was shared with teachers to demonstrate how children simplify messages so that meaning exists without complexity of statement.

Next, the Interactive Language Development Teaching format developed by Lee, Koenigsnecht and Mulhern (1974), although designed to teach adult syntactic constructions of increasing complexity, can also be used at the semantic–grammatical rule level of language instruction. Instead of complete sentences (with functors and inflections), the clinician can model semantic–grammatical rules and combinations of these rules. For example:

Clinician: Ernie is going shopping at Mr. Hopper's store. *Ernie shop.* What is Ernie doing?
Child: Ernie shop.
Clinician: Ernie tells Mr. Hooper, "I want an apple." Ernie wants an apple. *Ernie want apple.* Tell me what Ernie wants.
Child: Ernie want apple.

In addition, the Lee, Koenigsnecht and Mulhern (1974) Interactive format can be used to improve auditory memory and comprehension skills:

1. Programming for auditory memory deficits can be incorporated into expressive language development, by using the Interactive teaching strategy. Since the clinician models the correct sentence construction, the child must listen, remember the modeled sentence, and repeat it in response to the clinician's question or eliciting statement (see above example). While the authors note that verbatim repetition is not necessary (except for the target structure) during the language lesson, the clinician could require verbatim responses to build auditory memory skills. It is possible, for example, to construct an Individualized Educational Plan (IEP) such as "J will be able to repeat verbatim a modeled sentence of five to seven words with a DSS of ten to twelve within the Interactive Language Development Teaching format by . . . "

2. The author reported that listening comprehension was improved for a population of learning disability children when they were able to interact verbally with story characters and plot details rather than remaining passive listeners (Simon 1978). In other words, as the Interactive format was used, they entered into a dialogue about the story *while* the story was being told. Although data were not gathered, it might be speculated that the children were also exposed to separating significant details from peripheral story details by focusing on the types of content items that were modeled by the instructor. Perhaps this experience could serve as an intermediate step to becoming attentive and comprehending listeners. Additionally, as the story was told and sentences reworded, the students were exposed to various transformations of sentences within the story, helping them learn to decode the deep structure in various surface patterns.

An adaptation of a commercial program has been described by Simon (1979). Lipman, Sharp and Oscanyan (1977) developed a philosophy program for fifth grade children. Students follow characters in a "philosophical novel" through a series of thoughts and experiences that demonstrates one must not rely totally upon his or her perceptions or prejudices, but must call upon the principles of logic in order to reach sound conclusions. The goals of the program are to develop critical thinking and discussion skills. Learning/language disability children show deficiencies in both of these areas (Wiig and Semel 1976). The Lipman, Sharp and Oscanyan (1977) program was used by the author with adolescent learning disabled, emotionally handicapped boys who attended a "Philosophy Seminar" three times per week. Results of the study showed significant gains in deductive reasoning and discussion skills.

SUGGESTIONS FOR TRANSFERRING RESEARCH FINDINGS TO CLINICAL METHODOLOGY

Consider the following steps for incorporating new data into the clinical conceptual model of competent/incompetent communication as well as for refining evaluation and therapy strategies:

1. Formulate descriptive sectional titles for therapy, methodology, and clinical procedures, such as:
    a. normative data
    b. evaluation procedures
    c. programming ideas
    d. behavior management
    e. carryover

2. Peruse the professional literature for new developments and sort these data into the appropriate sectional titles listed above.

3. Sequence the data in each section from the most basic to the most advanced considerations.

4. Survey presently available and purchasable clinical materials to see how they could be used to implement your new knowledge.

5. Explore the versatility and limitations of the new information.

SUMMARY

Emphasis has been placed on (1) the importance of the clinician (and educator) formulating a conceptual model of "competent communication" versus "incompetent communication" skills, (2) engaging in continual refinement of evaluation and therapy procedures, and (3) exploring the versatility of theoretical and empirical contributions. Knowledge is advanced and refined through an interaction between research (theory) and clinical experience (application).

SECTION II
The Clinician's Conceptual Model
for Communicative Competence

INTRODUCTION

The author is in strong agreement with Rees (1978) that language clinicians need to keep syntactic training in proper perspective. Certainly if a child has not learned to order contentives (words that carry most of the meaning) and functors so that the form of his message conveys his communicative intent, he needs to rectify this difficulty. Additionally, if the complexity of the child's structure does not service the complexity of his thoughts, he can benefit from therapy that will focus on helping him combine and relate his thoughts. To reiterate, concentration on form alone is not language therapy. The purposes for and functions of communication as well as the conversational stylistic rules that maintain a "flow of meaning" (Rees 1978) and clarity of communicative intent deserve equal programming attention.

Dysfunctional communication calls attention to itself. Sometimes the reason for the dysfunctional impression is obvious and at other times is rather puzzling. The child who says "Her ain't my sister" is relying upon an objective pronoun rather than a subjective pronoun and using a colloquial negation form; the reason for the speaker's appearing "incompetent" is obvious. There are, however, some more subtle characteristics of incompetent communication. For example, the speaker's grammar may be adequate but it is difficult to comprehend his communicative intent. The discussion of possible reasons for this more puzzling type of incompetence is the focus of this section of the monograph.

If one compares a speaker's grammar to the "ideal" grammar described by the generative transformational model (Chomsky 1957), it is possible to focus precisely on the features of grammar that the speaker has internalized and those that he has not internalized. The author has found this an extremely useful clinical tool, especially as the model has been clinically applied by Hannah (1977) and Streng (1972). The generative transformational model, then, can serve as a guideline for analyzing a child's language *form*.

In an attempt to understand those more subtle features of incompetent communication, various theoretical models of proficient/nonproficient language *function* were consulted. The purpose of this section of the monograph is to consider three contributions, in particular, to the description of incompetent language *function and style:*

1. The fluency, coherence, and effectiveness and control displayed by a speaker affect the listener's impression of the speaker's competence (Loban 1961).

2. The degree of egocentricity displayed by the speaker affects the clarity of his communicative intent (Piaget 1955; Bernstein 1962, 1967).

3. For language to be a social and intellectual tool, the speaker must display communicative flexibility in many different contexts and roles (Halliday 1973, 1978; Bereiter and Engelmann 1966).

To be functional, language must "work" for an individual. "The individual is the configuration of a number of roles defined by the social relationships in which he enters. . . ." (Halliday 1978, p. 17). In other words, since we are not doing the same thing in the same place all of the time, language must shift to meet our contextual and role changes. In addition, language must be presented in such a manner that the listener can comprehend the communicative intent. Communication failure can usually be defined by the fact that the listener is attending to *how* the message is being sent rather than *what* the speaker is saying.

The purpose of a clinician's conceptual model of competent communication versus incompetent communication is to provide the "why's" for the "how to's" of programming. The model provides some explanations for the observation that the child's communication attempts are not working.

LOBAN'S CONSIDERATIONS OF COMMUNICATIVE COMPETENCE/INCOMPETENCE

Language proficiency develops through a sequence of attainments in form, function, and style. In a longitudinal study, Loban (1961) investigated the components of communication proficiency in a group of 338 kindergarten through sixth grade students in Oakland, California. In addition to general findings on the relationships between oral language/written language skill and socioeconomic status/oral and written language, he described some specific factors that accounted for differences in language proficiency. As the reader will note, form, function and style are all considered in Loban's (1961) model of language proficiency, and if the factors Loban has isolated are kept in mind by the language clinician, there is little chance that language therapy will consist only of syntax training. Each of the factors Loban has isolated will be considered separately.

Fluency

Fluency refers to the ability to find words with which to express oneself and to do so readily. In Loban's study he looked at the degree of skill development in three groups: random, low–language–proficiency, and high–language–proficiency. The low–proficiency group said less and had more trouble saying it — a very similar description to that of Blue's (1975) for the "marginal communicator." There was less vocabulary, with repetition of the same words when more precise vocabulary would have better served their needs. [It would be interesting to know whether or not this vocabulary restriction was due to a "competence factor" or a "performance factor" in light of Morehead and Johnson's (1972) notation on the lack of creativity displayed by language deficient children in *using* the knowledge of language structure that they do possess. Perhaps they also fail to use vocabulary they "know."] There was a more expansive vocabulary, more precision in word choice, more variety of statement, and freedom from false starts (or mazes — which will be discussed under "coherence") for the high proficiency group. The low group, it seemed, had more difficulty formulating a response as well as difficulty gaining control over English syntax patterns. Due to these factors, they got involved in more mazes.

Coherence

Coherence refers to the ability to organize the content of the message prior to its delivery. Loban (1961) discusses three basic types of coherence that mark the proficient language user.

Coherence through the use of subordinating clauses and connectors (such as although, because, and unless) refers to the ability to subordinate some ideas to others, thus avoiding a haphazard, unsystematic way of uttering or "sputtering" perceptions and thoughts. Through clauses and connectives, the speaker can sequence details and relationships among details. Differences between Loban's high and low proficiency groups revealed that, except for a loose chronology, the low group lacked coherence and emphasis necessary to successfully communicate content. They were not, for example, fully aware of how dependent clauses could be used as a way to communicate ideas in relation to each other. However, Loban cautions the clinician to observe the quality and not just the quantity of dependent clauses; complex sentences can sometimes reflect confusion rather than control. In other words, analysis might reflect that some complex sentences could actually be improved by being recast as simple sentences. The more proficient speaker seems to have an intuitive grasp of when to employ a simple statement and when to interrelate several statements. In addition to adequate subordination used by the high group, there was consistent use of infinitives, participial phrases, gerunds, appositives, and nominals. Study results supported Loban's hypothesis that the complexity of grammatical structure is associated not only with chronological age, but also with language proficiency. The study indicated, then, that while the low proficiency group operated primarily at the phrase structure grammatical level (which generates simple, active kernel statements), the high group had at its command an array of transformations with which to manipulate the kernel structures to produce varying degrees of complexity.

Coherence through the control of "mazes" refers to the ability to plan and sequence a message so that there are few repetitions of words and phrases. When mazes are not controlled, fluency is affected and communication is less effective because the listener has difficulty following the flow of meaning. Loban (1961) generally found that the number of mazes per language sample decreased with age, especially after third grade. Although there was a considerable variance within the low group and its ability to control mazes at any age, the high group, in contrast, controlled mazes by holding them down to just a few words. Consider the difference in control among these three examples of mazes offered by Loban (1961, p. 25):

Transcription	Communication Units	No. of Words in Mazes
1. (Short maze at the beginning of a communication unit and integrally related to that communication unit) ["I'm goin] ... I'm goin' to build a flying saucer/but I can't think how yet."	2	3
2. (Short maze in the middle of a communication unit and integrally related to that communication unit.) "When I was fixin' ready to go home, my mother called me up in the house/an' [an' an' have to] I have to get my hair combed."	2	4
3. (Long maze not immediately related to a communication unit. The child apparently drops the whole project as being too complicated for his powers.) "I saw a hunter program last Sunday/[an' he, an' snow time he had to have lot uh, wah-h when he, uh, not too many dogs, he . . .] /and that's all I think of that picture."	2	18

Lack of coherence through excessive mazes and lack of subordination will receive further attention in Section IV, which is devoted to examples of nonproficient communication. At this point, it is hoped that the reader has a sensitivity to the "maze" as an important factor in communication competence (or the lack of it!).

Coherence of spoken style refers to the general ease with which communication is formulated and to the distinctness of speech. How easy is it to listen to this person and comprehend the meaning of his message? There is a communicative reciprocity enjoyed between the speaker and the listener; the degree of listener attentiveness is usually related to how easy the speaker is to listen to. It is difficult, for example, to continue a dialogue with an individual who cannot sustain the topic, rambles, or speaks in a slurred or rapid manner. These speaker–listener roles are currently being focused upon in the study of the pragmatic aspects of communication. It appears that the development of discourse (defined as the ability to share the same topic and add information to the prior utterance from someone else) matures in adult-child contexts prior to child-child contexts (Rees 1978). Gelman and Shatz (1977), however, observed that by age four, children demonstrate an impressive ability to stay on the topic when it is related to instruction — especially when telling a younger listener how an object works.

When a clinician finds a ten- to twelve-year-old who is still having difficulty in being an effective communicator of instructions and/or in keeping in the topic of conversation, it is imperative that his marginal communicating skills be considered clinically; he may or may not have adequate syntactic form, but this is quite apart from the efficacy of including him in the case load. His IEPs can focus on the pragmatic aspects of communication.

Effectiveness and Control

Effectiveness and control refers to the degree of development among form, function, and style; it is the interaction of all three. Variables include: a purposeful order displayed by the ability to use various structural patterns, mastery of conventional usage and grammar, ability to express tentative thinking by means of provisional or conditional statements (such as could, should, might, perhaps, and if/then), coherence in the use of subordination and connectives, and the control of mazes. For the low proficiency group in Loban's (1961) study, there was more substitution of word groups for single words ("the guy that fixes cars" for "mechanic," for example) and less variety in choice and arrangement of movable syntactic elements (such as adjectival, adverbial or prepositional phrases) as well as in the structuring of noun and verb phrases. Basically, the higher group demonstrated more creativity in their use of oral language. While there was little difference in the use of embedding *phrases,* the high group consistently showed greater use of *clauses* and *multiples* (movables within movables, such as "whoever [in the excitement] manages to keep from laughing"). In addition, a sensitivity to subject-predicate agreement appeared related to overall language skill. The use of conditional and tentative thinking structures, supposition, and formation of hypotheses occurred more frequently with the high group, and Loban (1961) found in his longitudinal study that the high group had used language in this way from kindergarten. In other words, from approximately the time researchers have indicated that child language has most of the adult language properties (age five to six), the high proficiency group made optimal use of the grammar to express themselves and did so with ease.

As Wiig and Semel (1976) have pointed out, children with language disabilities do not seem to *perceive* many of the language nuances (such as the difference in meaning among could, should, might, may have been). If no difference in meaning is perceived, it is not surprising that they (or perhaps the children of Loban's low proficiency group) would not use these structures; from a very early age, meaning appears to dictate choice of words during communication efforts (Schlesinger 1971). It is also possible that the intertwining of cognitive and linguistic skills might be responsible for the absence of multiples. Perhaps Loban's low proficiency group was unable to attend to multiple factors at once; or consider, if they could have attended (or being *taught* to attend) to multiple factors, they still might not have developed the structural knowledge to express these in combinations (Furth and Youniss 1976).

Obviously, one's control over structure and vocabulary would have direct relevance to one's communicative effectiveness. A person who is comfortable with the language system and its supportive vocabulary will be able to manipulate appropriate degrees of complexity in a facile manner to express himself fluently and coherently in a variety of contexts. When a child is referred to the language clinician with a teacher comment such as "He gets all mixed up whenever he tries to tell me something, and I have difficulty understanding what he is trying to say," it is imperative that the clinician create tasks that survey the factors Loban (1961) has isolated: (1) How well can the child describe an object or explain how an appliance works, or relate sequentially his morning schedule? (2) Can he tell you about a movie or a television program he saw so that the details are coherently sequenced? (3) Is he able to carry on a conversational dialogue with the clinician? (4) Is his voice audible and his speech intelligible? (5) What percentage of his sentences (in the language sample) contain mazes, and how many words are involved in most of the mazes? (6) Does he show mazes in one context (such as giving instructions or explanations) more than in another?

Evaluative observations of a child's fluency, coherency, and effectiveness and control will focus on the factors that are largely responsible for a "marginal communicator" being referred to the language clinician. See Appendix 11 for a checklist developed by Loban (1961). This is an excellent summary of proficient to nonproficient communication skills viewed on a continuum. It is recommended that the clinician have copies of this available to classroom teachers so that the marginal communicators can be recognized, referred, and included in communication programming.

Pragmatic Considerations

Related to Loban's (1961) model of language proficiency is the notion of "the speech act," a term Rees (1978) mentions as most closely associated with the work of John Searle (1969). It is Searle's hypothesis that speech acts and not sentences are the basic or minimal units of linguistic communication. Searle notes four types of speech acts (discussed at some length in Rees 1978) that are not mutually exclusive; rather, they should be thought of as a description of what is going on when a speaker says something to a listener. For example, a sentence's *illocutionary* speech act refers to the way in which the speaker intends for his utterance to be interpreted by the listener. Rees (1978) offers some examples of this (p. 200):

Utterance	Illocutionary Act
You were right about the mosquitoes.	admitting
This chowder is delicious.	evaluating
Please take out the garbage.	requesting
Shoot when you see the whites of their eyes.	commanding

Perlocutionary speech acts, then, refer to the *actual* effects that the illocutionary speech acts have on the listener in modifying his behaviors or beliefs. "It is obvious that the illocutionary acts depend more upon the speaker's intentions and the conditions and context of the speaking than on the syntactic form of the spoken sentence" (Rees 1978, p. 201).

Not only can an entire dialogue be calculated to produce certain listener results, but any single sentence can be viewed as the minimal unit of the dialogue in terms of its effect upon the listener. The command one has of language structure, fluency of expression, coherence of organization, and clarity of spoken style can all have direct bearing upon whether an illocutionary act becomes a perlocutionary act. In other words, how effective is the speaker in communicating his intent? A listener's response may automatically comment on the speaker's "communicative competence." Granted, the listener may have receptive processing difficulties, but the focus of this monograph is on the *speaker's* communicative competence.

EGOCENTRICITY

Piaget's Observations

The next major consideration in establishing a conceptual model for communicative competence is the role of egocentricity in communication. Piaget, in *The Language and Thought of the Child* (1955) concluded that there are two major categories of speech:

1. *Egocentric speech:* speech that, whether uttered in solitude or the presence of others, can be judged to lack a primary communicative intent (there is no real attempt to take the role of the listener or to adapt the message to his informational needs).

2. *Socialized (sociocentric) speech:* speech that appears to possess genuine communicative aims.

Piaget's research indicated that until a child is approximately seven years old, it is difficult for him to take the perspective of another person in a physical or social situation. The world revolves around the small child, and he assumes that the listener knows the sequence and/or the antecedents of events about which he is speaking. In addition, the child sees no need to justify his opinions because he assumes that everyone thinks the same way he does. The shift from egocentric to sociocentric thought occurs when it is discovered that others do not think as oneself. The child then adapts by recognizing the need for verification and, in doing so, replaces egocentric logic with true logic. This gradual transfer occurs, according to Piaget, because thought is becoming more socialized. (The child's social–linguistic interactions account, in part, for the transition toward logical thought that occurs during the Concrete Operational stage [Sigel and Cocking 1977]).

In one experiment with children in the very early grades, Piaget gave some information to one child and asked him to relate this information to a second child of the same age. He came to two conclusions after viewing their behaviors:

1. Children of this age do not communicate material very clearly because (in their egocentrism) they fail to adapt to the role of the listener and his needs.

2. As listeners, they do not process information very well that is presented by the speaker (Dale 1976).

Piaget's investigations convinced him that egocentrism is a pervasive characteristic of cognition in the pre–school years and still evident in the first couple of years in school. Gestures and ambiguous pronouns are extensively used by the young child, who seems unaware that there are other points of view in addition to his own. Piaget found much greater egocentrism in children's speech directed to adults than in speech to other children. In other words, the children seemed to assume that adults just automatically "understand." This would indicate that the child really *is* somewhat aware that certain modifications can be made depending upon the audience, and this has, indeed, been substantiated by current research.

Related Research

In a study by de Villiers and de Villiers (1974), it was observed that 2½–year–old and 4½–year–old children demonstrated abilities to behave nonegocentristically in giving directions for finding a hidden piece of candy. All but the youngest children did better on these tasks than Piaget's conceptions of egocentricity would predict, which led the researchers to conclude that young children may not be as egocentric as Piaget's conclusions would imply — at least on tasks of similar complexity.

"Communicative planning" begins at the one-word stage, according to research by Greenfield and Smith (1976). If a child wants a truck, he might say "wanna" if there is just one toy in his midst. However, the child is more likely to verbalize "truck" if there are alternative toys available. The quality of "informativeness" seems to guide word selection. The Greenfield and Smith (1976) data suggest that very young children do make presuppositions (or assumptions) in some contexts about what information is or is not in the listener's consciousness. Bates (1976) believes that these assumptions guide even pre-linguistic behaviors (such as gestures, crying). Regardless of age, evidence suggests that illocutionary speech acts are attempting to prompt the desired perlocutionary speech acts. For this to happen, ". . . it is clear that the speaker must make assumptions continually about what information is and is not shared between himself and his listener. When the speaker's assumptions are correct, the sentences will be comprehensible as intended. When the speaker's assumptions are incorrect, the sentences do not work as intended and communication fails" (Rees 1978, p. 205).

Shatz and Gelman (1973), in light of the most recent research on a child's ability to consider his listener at an early age, stress that any measurement of a child's ability to communicate information should be conducted under circumstances where the cognitive tasks do not exceed his abilities; otherwise, the test becomes one of cognitive rather than communicative skills.

Restricted Versus Elaborated Codes

Background

Bernstein (1964, 1967) studied the effects of social class on the use of the restricted versus the elaborated codes. The emphasis in this monograph, however, is not within this limited socio-linguistic context. Instead, attention is directed to why communication appears competent or incompetent, regardless of the speaker's socioeconomic status. Bernstein has isolated the variable of "assumptions." He described communicative effectiveness on a continuum, depending upon whether or not the speaker was assuming accurately the amount of information shared by himself and the listener.

Bernstein began in the early 1960s with the observation that educational failure was not distributed randomly in the population, but tended to correlate with social class; the lower the family on the social scale, the greater the child's chances of failure. The "code theory" was developed to try to account for linguistic differences between social classes. Differences in code were considered relative; they are tendencies or orientations within each individual that display considerable variation (Halliday 1978).

Restricted Code

A "restricted code," according to Bernstein, is a highly contextually-based use of language, involving a high frequency of idioms and cliches to express global concepts. In addition, there is an extensive use of elliptical references to shared (or assumed to be shared) knowledge and frequent substitution of pronouns for more descriptive nouns. In other words, the restricted code is highly contextually bound, with the speaker assuming that the listener has had the same experiences and impressions as he has had. The restricted code emerges when the individual makes a "we" assumption. "Communication goes forward against a backcloth of closely shared identifications and effective empathy which removes the need to elaborate verbal meaning and logical continuity in the organization of speech" (Bernstein 1970, p. 32). The use of a restricted code creates social solidarity at the cost of the verbal elaboration of individual experience. When operating on a "we" assumption, then, the speaker assumes that the listener only needs to have bits of information to "jog the memory," rather than a chronology of explicit details. While the restricted code may be entirely appropriate for certain contexts, role switching in the culture requires that more explicit forms of communication also be available.

"The restricted code is *not* equated with linguistic deprivation. . . . [The person who relies on this code] possesses the same tacit understanding of the linguistic system as any child. It simply means that there is a restriction on the contexts and on the conditions which will orient the child to universalistic orders of meaning — as contrasted to meaning derived solely from personal experience — and to making those linguistic choices through which such meanings are realized and so made public. It does not mean that the child cannot produce at *any* time elaborated speech in particular contexts" (Bernstein 1970, p. 56).

Elaborated Code

An "elaborated code," in principle, presupposes a sharp boundary or gap between self and others (Bernstein 1970). The speaker focuses on the fact that his experiences are different from those of his listener and searches for a way to make the listener understand his experiences. It is making an "I" assumption; I have experienced this event, but I assume that you have not. The elaborated code, therefore, is a highly explicit contextually–independent version of the same language, involving expressions that are interpretable in a variety of contexts without a great deal of prior knowledge about speakers, listeners, and speech setting. "In general, the ability to use language in abstract and indirect contexts of situations is what distinguishes the speech of adults from that of [small] children; learning language consists in part in learning to free it from the constraints of the immediate environment" (Halliday 1978, p. 29). According to Bernstein (1970, p. 32):

> an elaborated code will arise whenever the intent of the other person cannot be taken for granted; speakers are forced to elaborate their meanings and make them both explicit and specific. Meanings which are discreet and local to the speaker must be [formulated] so that they are intelligible to the listener. This pressure forces the speaker to select among syntactic alternatives and encourages differentiation of vocabulary.

Among those children and adolescents who relied heavily upon the "restricted code," Bernstein observed rigidity of syntactic organization, *relative* to those who switched from the restricted to the elaborated code when the context demanded it. In those who flexibly moved between the codes, he noted more passives, more complex verbs, and a greater proportion of subordinate clauses. There are, then, both differences in the form and the number of explicit references in the elaborated code.

Comparative Uses of the Two Codes

Bernstein (1970) emphasizes that the different "codes" refer to performance rather than competence; in other words, as Ervin–Tripp (cited in Bernstein 1970, p. 94) cautions: "We have to be very wary of developing a mythology about differences in communicative *competence*. . . . When [the person] is told what is required, differences disappear."

Actually, Bernstein is not implying that there are two *separate* codes. The terms "restricted" and "elaborated" refer to opposite poles on a continuum from implicit to explicit uses of the same language. They are different strategies of language use, based upon the speaker's interpretation of what the situation demands (Halliday 1978). The advantage of the restricted code is its economy; if and when the speaker *can* assume a great deal of shared information, the restricted code is more efficient. The elaborated code is preferable when the speaker knows very little about his listener and the particular setting in which messages are exchanged (Bates 1976). Communicative effectiveness seems to depend upon the facility with which the individual can switch from the restricted to the elaborated code. This switching is based on making new assumptions with each listener and in each context — or, as Osser (1969) states, "the ability to analyze the listener's role characteristics." Table 2 reviews the different characteristics of the two codes.

TABLE 2

Summary of Differences Between the Elaborated and Restricted Codes

Restricted	Elaborated
1. Implicit statement of fact and intent.	1. Explicit statement of fact and intent.
2. Less time taken to plan the sequence of statements and logical relationships to be communicated.	2. A coherence of expression suggests mental planning prior to statement.
3. Speech is fast and articulation frequently sloppy.	3. Articulation does not impede listener comprehension of individual words selected.
4. Involves a basic (low) level of syntactic and vocabulary selection.	4. Appropriate variety of syntax and vocabulary is present, which adequately maps the speaker's intentions with precision and appropriate complexity of intertwining relationships.
5. Speaker assumes common experiences with the listener.	5. Speaker focuses on the experiences of others as different from his own.
6. Reliance upon the extra–verbal channels during message transmission.	6. Orientation toward the verbal channel.
7. Limited use of language to verbally explore possibilities or conceptual alternatives.	7. A range of possibilities is verbally explored within a complex conceptual hierarchy.

The School Code

While reliance upon the restricted code works well within the home setting and, to a certain extent, within the neighborhood, it places those children who rely heavily upon it at a disadvantage in the school setting. This is particularly evident when written communication is required, because the reader is unable to ask clarifying questions, such as a listener can in conversation. As Halliday (1978) and Moore (1971) point out, education demands an elaborated code much of the time.

Addressing himself to the contextual adaptations that a speaker needs to make, Moore (1971, p. 19) notes:

> A child may possess a certain syntactic structure as evidenced by its presence at several places in a large sample of his speech, but may not be able to use it in a specific situation. Or he may possess a basic rule (e.g., for the formation of a basic noun–adjective combination) but be unable to apply the rule recursively when the situation demands a greatly elaborated set of adjectives to specify a particular object accurately.

Moore (1971) suggests two broad types of situational influences on language performance, which he characterizes as "social" and "cognitive" in terms of the demands of the situation. Social demands include such variables as the status and roles of the conversants, their attitudes toward language communication, and their motives in a particular speech interaction. Cognitive demands include such factors as the complexity of speech required to communicate a given message, the extent to which one can rely upon "props" within the situation to ease the burden of communication, and the difficulty of the vocabulary required for communicating a given message. Obviously, cognitive demands (such as those occurring in the classroom) require an elaborated code. (This topic will be discussed in the section entitled "Flexibility in Language Functions," page 33.)

Moore (1971, p. 21) concludes that the following set of cognitive demands would require an elaborated code:

1. when speakers cannot rely on previously accumulated, shared information;
2. when the speaker is required to take his listener into account by specifically naming referents that are not present or about which the listener lacks information;
3. when the bulk of the communication load falls on the language code itself, as opposed to such extra-linguistic activities such as pointing and voice intonation.

Based upon a review of sociolinguistic research, Moore (1971, p. 37) outlined a compensatory program to develop a code that would more appropriately meet the social and cognitive demands of the school setting. This outline appears as Appendix 15.

Pragmatic Considerations on Roles and Contexts

Studies stimulated by a new interest in pragmatics have focused on this general area of speaker adaptability. In addition to the research cited earlier of de Villiers and de Villiers (1974) and Greenfield and Smith (1976) showing what appears to be a conscious concern in quite young children that the listener comprehend their messages, Shatz and Gelman (1973) observed stylistic variations in four-year-olds as they spoke to two-year-olds. Gleason's (1973) research showed that by age eight children have three styles of speaking: to each other, to babies, and to adults. Gleason also noted that they talk differently to parents (more request-demand oriented) than to adults outside the family (more conversationally oriented). "It is clear that children (like adults) do demonstrate considerable (if variable) sensitivity to the listener's ability to comprehend" (Rees 1978, p. 248).

Continuing with the consideration of interactions and expectations occurring during discourse, Katz and Langedoen (1976) explain that the language user's pragmatic skills make it possible for him to exploit information about an utterance context to achieve utterance meaning beyond that assigned to the sentence by the grammar alone. An example might be "You keep your house quite warm," meaning "Would you please reset the thermostat so that I can be cooler and more comfortable?" Ervin-Tripp (1977) refers to this as "tactful deviousness" and notes that a child's understanding of such statements is a rather late accomplishment. A speaker makes a "tactfully devious" remark like the one above on the assumption that the listener will "read between the lines."

Assumptions seem to play a major role in speaker-listener interactions. Certainly, egocentric messages are sent with the assumption that the listener knows everything the speaker knows. What about the conversational assumptions that are made? Grice (1975) has identified four rules (and subrules) that speakers and listeners expect in the cooperative venture of dialogue:

1. Quantity (the quantity of information to be provided)
   a. Make the contribution as informative as is needed (for the current purposes of the exchange).
   b. The contribution should not be more informative than is required, or the speaker appears effusive.
2. Quality (try to make a truthful contribution)
   a. Do not say what you do not believe.
   b. Do not say that for which you lack adequate evidence.
3. Relation (be relevant to the ongoing topic)
4. Manner (be easily understood; clear in meaning)
   a. Avoid obscurity of expression.
   b. Avoid ambiguity.
   c. Be brief.
   d. Be orderly.

According to Grice (1975), when the speaker fails to observe any of these rules, the listener starts trying to figure out the speaker's implied meaning. "Older children and adults engage in 'repair mechanisms' that modify and restate prior utterances until the referent is established" (Rees 1978, p. 242).

It would be clinically responsible to not only probe the child's adaptive capabilities during evaluation, but to teach "message clarification" strategies (or "repair mechanisms") as one of the pragmatic reasons for using various question forms as well as precise vocabulary.

No research findings and implications on speaker-listener interactions are more dramatic than those that have been completed on "referential skills." As Brown (1958) noted, referents (whether objects, events, or relationships) do not have single names. For example, "food" can be referred to as edibles, grub, chow, morsels, sustenance, or snack. A speaker has considerable latitude in the name he selects. Choice of words is partially determined by the set of alternatives from which he must distinguish the intended referent. (Recall the earlier cited research of Greenfield and Smith, 1976, on children's vocabulary choice at the one-word level.)

When looking at communicative effectiveness and the degree of socialized (or non-egocentric) speech necessary, a certain flexibility is essential; one must be as precise as the situation demands. A pencil in a box of marbles can be called "pencil"; however, in a collection of pencils, "pencil" alone would be inadequate. The speaker might need to employ a phrase such as "the four-inch blue pencil." By objectively considering the informational needs of the listener, a shift toward specificity is made along the restricted to elaborated code continuum. "The difficult cognitive task for the speaker is to consider the set of alternatives from which the listener must select the intended referent and to provide the listener with the appropriate information" (Dale 1976, p. 256).

Referential Skills

Glucksberg, Krauss and Weisberg (1966) and Glucksberg and Krauss (1967) studied referential skills. They set up game situations to assess the ability of children and adults to communicate a single referent. Two children or adults were seated at a table, separated by an opaque screen. Each had a collection of six blocks on the table before him. Each block had a distinctive, novel line drawing. The drawings were designed to be difficult to name but relatively easy to distinguish. One subject, the decoder, selected one block at a time from the set of six on the basis of a verbal message (a description) provided by the other subject, the encoder. While adult performance on this task was nearly perfect, a 50 percent success level (in describing the line drawings to the listener) was not attained among the children until they reached approximately seventh grade.

Although pre-school children understood the game and could play as long as the referents were easy to describe (such as colored blocks or animals), their selection of the blocks with novel drawings was random. An example of extreme egocentrism in the kindergarten population was the child (the encoder) who said, "This one," and received a reply from the decoder, "Do you mean that one?" The reply was "Yes." (Of course, the opaque screen was obstructing visual contact so demonstratives such as "this" or "that" were meaningless!) Glucksberg, Krauss and Weisberg (1966) and Glucksberg and Krauss (1967), like Piaget, noted that the children *assumed* that they were communicating even when, in reality, they were not.

It would appear that there are various degrees of egocentrism and ability to process explanations, depending upon the nature of the task and the information exchanged therein. For example, while four-year-old children might be able to give directions that would be clear enough for someone to process in finding hidden candy (de Villiers and de Villiers 1974), describing an abstract line drawing with sufficient precision to enable a listener to identify a duplicate of it proved to be a difficult task for seventh graders.

When children were given adult messages, their selections were more accurate; children were, then, better decoders than encoders. This is not surprising considering that receptive skills consistently seem to develop ahead of expressive skills. Encoding may be the more difficult task because it not only requires the selection of appropriate distinctive features of an object, but also an organized, coherent message relating these.

A particularly striking difference between children and adults on this series of referential tasks was shown by their respective reactions to feedback from the decoder about his own understanding. When the decoder might say "I don't understand which one you mean," adult encoders were likely to provide completely new descriptions or to elaborate previous messages, based upon their analysis of possible ambiguities present in their earlier message. Children, on the contrary, were more likely to simply repeat the original descriptions or just remain silent, probably assuming that since they had told "the truth," the listener had just not "heard." These findings would imply that Grice's (1975) four rules for cooperative conversation could not be readily manipulated by young children in an attempt to respond to listener requests for additional information.

There is no reason why the clinician could not occupy the role of negotiator in a task similar to that described by Glucksberg, Krauss and Weisberg (1966) and Glucksberg and Krauss (1967). In such a role, the clinician could help the encoder recognize the types of information a listener needs and could guide the decoder in asking clarification questions. For example (using toy objects):

Encoder: Put the chair beside the block.
Clinician: (helping the encoder) Did you say *which* side?
Encoder: Put the chair on the right side of the block. Now, put the lamp behind the block.
Clinician: (helping the decoder) Do you know *how far* behind the block you should put the lamp?
Decoder: How far behind the block should I put the lamp?
Encoder: Put it about one inch behind the block.

This type of analysis presents an opportunity for children to develop more socialized communication skills as well as to develop use of the elaborated code. It can also aid in developing more effective evaluative skills; the speaker will be able to evaluate how well his message construction has considered the listener's point of view, and the listener can learn to evaluate when he needs additional information to successfully complete a task. There might be occasions when the clinician would not want to permit any questioning. For example, if a student persists in relying upon clarification questions rather than organizing a nonegocentric message, it would be wise to construct an IEP such as "J. will provide sufficiently clear *unprompted* directions, so that a listener will be able to reproduce in four out of five trials a relationship between two objects that J. has constructed."

Referential tasks such as those just described make all of the cognitive demands delineated by Moore (1971) on pages 29-30 of this monograph. This means, of course, that it is absolutely necessary to make use of the elaborated code. The author has found that using the tasks described in these studies on referential skills is an ideal way to introduce the concept of "listener needs" to children. The novel line drawings are too difficult, but placement of objects in relation to each other works exceedingly well as a beginning step. It is recommended that the clinician assemble *pairs* of blocks and dollhouse furniture that can be used for this exercise. Inexpensive packages of each are available at grocery and discount stores.

FLEXIBILITY IN LANGUAGE FUNCTIONS

Introduction

One of the dominant concerns of the preceding section was the child's ability to keep his listener in mind during all message–sending. Now let's turn to the various reasons that would prompt an individual to communicate, keeping in mind that regardless of the function that language is meant to serve, the output needs to relate the communicative intent through clear referents in a fluent and coherent manner. These factors will have bearing upon the effectiveness of the message regardless of the purpose or context.

There is a gradual widening of the range of adaptation of a child's language. "The child who is going to move out into the world, as children do, must learn to make his speech broadly and flexibly adaptive" (Brown 1973, p. 245). We expect a lot from language. As Halliday (1978, p. 21) enumerates, we expect the linguistic code to:

1. reduce phenomena of the world into classes;

2. express logical relations (and . . ., or . . ., if . . .);

3. express our various roles and the wishes, feelings, attitudes, and judgments we have in each of these roles; and

4. possess formulation possibilities that can encode novel experiences for us in discourse.

Demonstrating "language flexibility" means that an individual effectively communicates in a variety of roles and contexts; the individual moves with ease from one language to another. "Language functions" simply refer to the fact that people engage in a variety of social actions and use language in each. Therefore, language is not just a system of rules — it is a resource. It has meaning potential (Halliday 1978). When we focus on the processes of human interaction, we are seeing this meaning potential at work.

The research and observations of Halliday (1973, 1975, 1978) and Bereiter and Engelmann (1966) will be considered as we discuss the nature of "language flexibility."

Halliday's Observations

Background

The child gradually learns how to mean; this is what initial language learning is — acquiring a range of meaning potential. "This consists in the mastery of a small number of elementary functions of language and a range of choices in meaning within each one" (Halliday 1978, p. 19). Each of the functions, then, expands internally. For example, the imaginative function of sound play develops into that of songs, rhymes, and stories.

Halliday (1973, 1975) adopts an integrative approach to studying how children make their speech "broadly and flexibly adaptive." He theorizes that language occupies the key role in socialization and learning, and that the very structural organization of language reflects the changing functions to which language is put from its earliest beginnings to its fully developed adult forms. In other words, language function guides its developing complexity of form.

If language is to be adequate for meeting the needs of the child, it has to be exhaustive and flexible; it must take account of the varied demands on language that the child will need to make. The different uses of language may be seen as realizing different intentions. As Halliday (1973) says, language is defined for the child by its uses; through its uses, language has meaning.

Although the various functions, in reality, can (and do) occur in combinations, each will be treated separately for purposes of defining and describing Halliday's model of child language functions.

Seven Child Language Functions

Halliday's seven functions of language for the child (or models of language the child constructs through experience) are described below:

1. *Instrumental* refers to language used to satisfy material needs ("I want . . ."). The child becomes aware that language can be used as a means of getting things done; it can manipulate and control the environment.

2. *Regulatory* refers to language used to control behavior ("do as I tell you"). This is closely related to the instrumental function in that the child learns that others use language to control him. Through his awareness of how people use language to control him, he attempts to use it similarly to control peers and siblings. These early uses provide the basis for the child's language of rules and instructions; demands progress to sequences of instructions and further progress to converting sets of instructions into rules, including conditional rules such as those used in explaining the principles of a game.

3. *Interactional* refers to language used in attempts to get along with others ("me and you"). Language used in the interaction between self and others is closely related to the regulatory function, but here it is used in social interaction. Language is used to define and consolidate a group and impose status and degree of group inclusion and acceptance.

4. *Personal* refers to language used to express self–identity ("here I come"). It is the individual's use of language to offer something unique and make public his individuality. There is direct expression of feelings and attitudes. The personal and interactional functions are related in the sense that the self is shaped through interactions with others.

5. *Heuristic* refers to the use of language to learn and explore reality ("tell me why"). Through questioning, the child seeks facts, explanations of facts, and generalizations about reality. Understanding the nature of "questions" and "answers," as well as "knowing" and "understanding," help the child to talk about his world and his place in it and to do so without difficulty. Parent–child heuristic interactions are significant to the child's later success in formal education.

6. *Imaginative* refers to when language is used for a creative formation of reality ("let's pretend"). There appears a linguistically created environment in which things are not as they really are, but as the child feels inclined to have them.

7. *Informational (or representational)* refers to the use of language to communicate content ("I've got something to tell you"). The child learns that he can convey a message through language that has specific reference to the processes, persons, objects, abstractions, qualities, states, and relations of the real world around him. This is not one of the earliest functions to appear or gain prominence; this function, for the child, is quite an unrealistic picture of language, since it accounts for only a small fragment of his total awareness of what language is all about. School, however, demands that it becomes a larger and larger fragment.

Relationship Between Language Flexibility and School Success

Halliday expresses concern about the failure of children to perform well in the school setting. "Bernstein has shown that educational failure is often, in a very general and rather deep sense, language failure" (Halliday 1973, p. 18). According to Halliday, it is likely that it is not "reading" and "writing" that Bernstein (1964, 1965) has pegged, but a deeper and more general problem of the fundamental mismatch between the child's linguistic capabilities and the demands that are made upon them.

The teacher operates on the assumption, or takes for granted, that by the time a child arrives at school, language is a means of learning. This is an assumption basic to the educational process. "In addition is the assumption that language is a means of personal expression and participation and is ready to be just *extended* to a new (school) context" (Halliday 1978, p. 31). In other words, it is necessary to know how to use language to learn and how to use language to participate as an individual in the learning situation. Halliday (1973) insists that the child who, in Bernstein's terms, has only a "restricted code" suffers some limitation because some of the functions of language have been developed one–sidedly. "The restriction is a restriction on the range of uses of language. In particular, he may not make unrestricted use of his linguistic resources in the two functions which are most crucial to his success in school: the personal and heuristic functions" (Halliday 1973, p. 18).

Programming Considerations

Halliday offers to instructors the following implications of his theoretical model of language functions:

1. The teacher's own model of language should not fall short of the child's (Halliday 1973).

2. The child's own linguistic experience should be considered, defining this experience in terms of its rich potential and noting where there may be differences of orientation that could cause the child difficulty in school (Halliday 1973).

3. The child's language development in school should have relevance to the linguistic demands that will be placed upon him in school and society (Halliday 1973). In other words, language teaching should emphasize text by concentrating upon:
   a. the rules of discourse.
   b. form, content, setting, participants, ends (intent and effect), key, medium, genre, and interactional norms (Hymes' components of speech).
   c. the determinants of speaking:
      (1) field = the ongoing activity and purposes that language is serving within the context;
      (2) tenor = interrelationships among participants (status and roles, for example);
      (3) mode = the style (didactic, fanciful, for example), the channel (written, spoken), and the purpose (to persuade, soothe, sell).
   d. extending the socializing contexts of language to include person–oriented interactional styles (Halliday 1978).

Halliday's theoretical position can best be summarized through a quotation from his book (1973, p. 20):

The child is surrounded by language, but not in the form of grammars and dictionaries or of randomly chosen words and sentences, or of undirected monologue. What he encounters is "test," or language in use; sequences of language articulated each within itself and with the situation in which it occurs. Such sequences are purposive — though very varied in purpose — and have an evident social significance. The child's awareness of language cannot be isolated from his awareness of language function, and this conceptual unity offers a useful vantage point from which language may be seen in a perspective that is educationally relevant.

35

Bereiter and Engelmann

Background

Bereiter and Engelmann's (1966) observations on the effects of limited language flexibility stem from their work with "disadvantaged" pre-school children. Their observations, however, are not just pertinent to, nor limited to, a particular socioeconomic group, but rather to children in general who do not show a functionally flexible use of their language knowledge.

Cognitive Uses of Language

Bereiter and Engelmann focus on the role of language in intellectual development. Language deficiencies of children who have difficulty in school do not seem to consist of deficiencies in vocabulary and grammar as such, but rather in the failure to master certain uses of language. While these children might have mastered language that is adequate for maintaining social relationships, and for meeting social and material needs, they have not mastered the use of language for obtaining and transmitting information, for monitoring one's own behavior, and for conducting verbal reasoning. What is lacking then, is mastery of the cognitive uses of language: to explain, describe, instruct, inquire, hypothesize, analyze, compare/contrast, deduce, and test. These are the uses that are necessary for academic success. Whenever a child appears to be having difficulty with "school language," it is recommended that his mastery of the cognitive uses of language be investigated.

Giant Words

A second aspect of Bereiter and Engelmann's (1966) description of inadequate verbal behavior is reliance upon "giant words," instead of distinct, meaningful units that compose a sentence. "The speech . . . seems to consist not of distinct words . . . but rather of whole phrases or sentences that function like giant words. . . . These giant word units cannot be taken apart by the child and recombined; they cannot be transformed from statements to questions, from imperatives to declaratives. . . ." (Bereiter and Engelmann 1966, p. 34). As an example, "This is a red truck," might sound like "Da-re-truh." It becomes incumbent upon the listener to interpret the meaning of the sound "ih" when it is used by the individual to represent "if," "it," "is," and "in." Bereiter and Engelmann state that this behavior is not just a matter of faulty pronunciation, but stems from the child's inability to deal with sentences as sequences of meaningful parts.

"[They] often blend the words together with noises that take the place of words and inflections they do not know, so that all the words tend to become fused into a whole. This leaves no distinctive units that can be recombined to generate new sentences" (Bereiter and Engelmann 1966, p. 36) Bernstein (1962) noted that the speech of ineffectively communicating adolescents he studied was characterized by large chunks of words that were treated as if they were single words, and while this led to a more rapid rate of speech, it also led to a less flexible use of language.

The author once again emphasizes that the clinician must not view Bereiter and Engelmann's observations of ineffective components of communication with "tunnel vision." The focus is on what makes an individual appear incompetent in communication. In the case of "giant words," intelligibility is impaired. Perhaps the reason for some of that unintelligibility is marginal familiarity with the meaningless functors or inflections that signal number, tense, and possession. In doubt, the child just glides over them, inserting an approximate syllabic unit. Regardless of whether the "giant words" are produced because of neurological constraints, lack of grammatical knowledge, or bad habit, a preponderance of these unintelligible constructions impedes communication; the listener is simply unable to decipher the communicative intent.

36

Verbal Reasoning

While Bereiter and Engelmann mention a general lack of mastery of the cognitive uses of language in children who tend to have difficulty in school, they specifically discuss difficulty in flexibly manipulating language as a system for investigation. This has an impact on the child's ability to use language deductively. They noted an inability to use the information gained from one set of verbal operations in subsequent operations. When faced with complex problems that cannot be solved except by a sequence of deductive steps, the student might say, "I don't know the answer to this one" rather than try to figure it out through the verbal statements available. An example would be a task such as found on the Inferences Subtest of the *California Test of Mental Maturity* (Sullivan, Clark and Tiegs 1961):

The box contains either gold or silver or crystal. It does not contain silver.
Therefore,
1. it contains crystal.
2. it contains either gold or crystal.
3. the conclusion is uncertain.

Three major tenets are basic to the Bereiter and Engelmann model of inflexible language skills:

1. By treating sentences as "giant words," an inflexible kind of language results that does not make full use of the potentialities of grammar and syntax and makes new vocabulary learning more difficult.

2. While social language is usually well established and effective, the cognitive uses of language, upon which the school setting focuses, have not been sufficiently developed.

3. There is a failure to focus on the integrity of each word and inflection in a statement, which severely limits the ability to use language for the manipulation of logical relationships.

Through viewing the Halliday (1973) and Bereiter and Engelmann (1966) models in tandem, we see with the first a description of the various language functions a child needs to . . . "move out into the world . . . and make speech broadly and flexibly adaptive" (Brown 1973, p. 245), and with the second, the kinds of deficits a child experiences who has had a "lop–sided" language development. Again, the author hopes that the reader will not view this information through a tunnel; it does *not* only relate to "culturally deprived" children. The scope is much more comprehensive: it includes most of those children who are "marginal communicators," regardless of their socioeconomic background or age.

Whether incompetent communication is caused by linguistic deficits, representational deficits, cognitive delays, or socioeconomic status is not the concern of this conceptual model. The emphasis is not on etiological explanations, but rather on behavioral description of those communication factors that inhibit communicative competence. The scope of the model is not restricted to an etiological explanation; it is more comprehensive. When faced with an ineffective, nonproficient, incompetent communicator, what are the *features* of his communication profile that produce this impression? The purpose of relating the theoretical concepts and empirical data in this section has been to isolate pertinent factors in incompetent communication strategies. Once isolated, developmental programming can be devised to strengthen each.

The purpose of the preceding section was to establish the conceptual model for *Communicative Competence: A Functional Pragmatic Approach to Language Therapy.* An attempt has been made to synthesize the theoretical and empirical information available that seems to describe the "incompetent" or "nonproficient" or "ineffective" communicator and to construct some ideas about what constitutes competent communication. From this information, behaviors contributing to ineffective communication can be more easily recognized during evaluation and it is possible to develop communication skills in therapy that will enable a child to perform with those attributes that seem to be characteristic of proficient communicators. A summary of major considerations seems in order.

SUMMARY:
INCOMPETENT COMMUNICATION FEATURES

There are many different types of incompetent language cases. Many programs have been devoted to developing syntax (Fristoe 1975), but structural difficulties are only a fragment of the communication problem that many children show. This conceptual model of competent versus incompetent communication views syntactic skill as only one component of a more comprehensive ability to *use* language effectively for any purpose, in any context, and in any role that arises. It is the composite of ineffective communication behaviors of the "marginal communicator" that has been explored in particular. This is the child for whom structural considerations alone neither describe his bizarre communicative patterns nor offer adequate goals for intervention. Many researchers, including Loban (1961), Bernstein (1962, 1964, 1967, 1970), Halliday (1973, 1975, 1978) and Bereiter and Engelmann (1966), have pinpointed some specific components of this ineffective communication style. Let's review the major observations:

1. There is an egocentric communication style due to referents that are not clear. The perspective of the listener is not taken into consideration when information or instructions are related.
    a. Age and background of the listener are not considered, so there is minimal (if any) adaptation of complexity (structure and vocabulary) relative to the listener's ability to comprehend.
    b. The proper amount of information (as much as is necessary to convey communicative intent) is frequently lacking.

2. Messages are characterized by static, uncreative structural patterns.
    a. The propensity for simple sentences does not allow details to be properly related through subordination.
    b. There are few nuances employed that differentiate subtle semantic moods and aspects (such as the meaningful differentiation between could, might, must, should, had been, have been).

3. There is very little planning of the message prior to its delivery.
    a. Experiences and events are not related sequentially, but rather uttered in freely associated thoughts, which makes the message sound incoherent.
    b. Fluency of expression is affected by many false starts while the speaker is deciding where to begin or how to structure the content, or searching for the "right word." Revisions possibly occur because the individual cannot seem to linguistically map his thoughts or because so many insignificant details are added that he loses his train of thought.

4. Carrying on a dialogue is a difficult task.
    a. There is difficulty maintaining the "flow of meaning" (or making comments that are directly relevant to the conversational topic).
    b. There is a cluttering of words, or sometimes slurred speech, which can lead to the listener making an inaccurate assumption about the speaker's intent.
    c. There is difficulty interpreting "tactfully devious" statements, which can lead to misunderstandings between the speaker and listener. A teacher, on the assumption that he is offering a polite and mature model for a child, might say, "Peanut butter all over the lunch table annoys me." He makes this statement on the assumption that the child will be able to infer the underlying meaning of his "tactfully devious" statement (i.e., "Next time, clean up the table after you have finished your lunch"). That assumption

can only be made, however, if the child is able to focus on not just the surface structure alone, but to survey the underlying meaning. Recognition of this possible problem with communication is particularly important in light of the widespread acceptance of Gordon's (1975) principles for parent and teacher effectiveness. Gordon suggests that the adult simply state how the child's behavior affects him; the child will then assume the responsibility for the modification of his behavior. These are "tactfully devious" comments, for the most part, from the adults.

5. The language system has not been molded to flexibly adapt to varying communication needs.
   a. While social uses of language are usually adequate, language used for cognitive and personal reasons is inadequate.
   b. The individual is not aware of the limitations of the restricted code; while it is efficient for use in social (and home) situations where there is mutual knowledge of events, the elaborate code needs to be retrieved for more intellectually oriented interactions among people from varying experiences.

6. Deficiencies in oral language affect other verbal modes of communication (i.e., reading and writing).
   a. Not being comfortable with words (and inflections) as single, movable units as well as more complex and interrelated syntactic statements, comprehension tends to be poor; this is especially evident after third grade when syntactic and semantic complexity are intertwined.
   b. Not being in a position to revise statements on the basis of immediate feedback or the clarity of the message, written work is poorly constructed and difficult to comprehend.

It is the philosophical position of this monograph that form, function, and style deserve equal attention from the language clinician. In addition, since individuals spend approximately twelve to sixteen years of their lives in a school setting, it is imperative that those aspects of communication that have an impact on academic and interpersonal performance in this setting receive preferential treatment.

SECTION III
Underlying Premises for
Communicative Competence (CC)

INTRODUCTION

Premises are constructed to state the philosophical and procedural bases for a particular position or argument. The author offers five premises that outline basic attitudes toward evaluation and therapy procedures:

1. The nature and extent of a language problem are defined by obtaining a sample of the language performance and by using correlate tests to supply additional descriptive data.

2. Evaluative data need to be organized for clinician analysis. The integrity of each linguistic component (phonology, morphology, syntax, and semantics) and interpersonal communication (coherent exchange of information) should be studied. Individualized Educational Plans (IEPs) should be constructed that enable programming to begin at the point of developmental disruption and to continue sequentially to the point of competence.

3. Therapy methodology should reflect the diversity of skill needs within one's caseload. Increased communication proficiency is intrinsically motivating and reinforcing. Realistic increments can be gradually achieved through task analysis and developmental programming.

4. Before new communication skills can become stabilized and generalized (or "carried over"), utterances must be unlaboriously produced in a variety of drill and meaningful situations.

5. Communication correlates (speaking, listening, reading, and writing) should not be artificially separated. Both readiness and reinforcement properties of each should be considered.

Since these premises serve as the superstructure for this functional–pragmatic approach to language evaluation and therapy, each will be explained.

PREMISE I

The nature and extent of a language problem are defined by obtaining a sample of the language performance and by using correlate tests to supply additional descriptive data.

Evaluation by the Clinician

It is critical to keep in mind that assessment is performed by the *clinician* — not by a battery of tests arbitrarily administered. To quote Siegel and Broen (1976, p. 75):

> The most useful and dependable language assessment device is an informed clinician who feels compelled to keep up with developments in psycholinguistics, speech pathology, and related fields and who is not slavishly attached to a particular model of language, or of assessment. In the long run, the attributes that will serve the clinician best are a willingness to explore new developments, to be experimental in approaching children and a persevering curiosity about the nature of language.

It is most efficient to begin with a focus on the *child* rather than a predetermined testing format. Disordered communication calls attention to itself because it is not functional. The clinician's responsibility is to answer the question, "What is the nature of this child's dysfunctional communication?" Just as therapy needs to be individualized, so does assessment. Each individual's communication behavior is measured against the clinician's theoretical conception of competent communication. In other words, when a clinician works from a theoretical conception about the nature of proficient language, there are intrinsic guidelines for the types of information (or observations) that should be gathered. All evaluation strategies should have an underlying purpose with respect to the individual and the conceptual model.

Receptive Evaluation

Evaluation of language reception should concentrate on how proficiently the child processes incoming cognitive–linguistic information. Wiig and Semel (1976) have proposed a logico–grammatical model to assess comprehension of agent–action–modifier–object–location constructions projecting intrinsic logical relationships among the words. The meaning of the words, inflections, and relationships among the words need to be assimilated by the listener for comprehension to occur. For example, "Although small, Jim was able to swiftly toss the large disc to the adjacent player," projects specific relationships among the words that would need to be deciphered by the listener. Who was small? What was large? Where was the disc thrown? To whom was the disc thrown? How was the disc thrown? As these words are processed in relation to each other, comprehension of the sentence occurs.

Rees and Shulman (1978) emphasize that focus on the *sentence* is not assessing comprehension; a series of sentences related to each other would be more representative of the type of comprehension necessary in discourse and reading. "A more inclusive orientation to the subject of the comprehension of spoken language would take into consideration a broad range of operations that the listener performs to obtain information from the heard utterance. The listener's operations may be grouped under three headings: (1) literal meaning, (2) presupposition and inference, and (3) illocutionary acts" (Rees and Shulman 1978, p. 209). Rees and Shulman suggest that the clinician incorporate listening comprehension tasks from reading readiness tests in the evaluation of the child's ability to understand the "total thought" being expressed in a series of related sentences. Akin to this is the child's ability to focus on the *topic* of discourse (Rees 1978), to answer questions appropriately, and to process multi–level instructions.

It should also be ascertained to what degree of accuracy the child can process an increasingly complex interaction between sophisticated syntax that is mapping challenging content (Lasky and Chapandy 1976). In other words, processing a series of simple sentences containing familiar vocabulary is quite different from technical vocabulary used in heavily embedded sentences. In evaluating comprehension performance, syntax, semantics, context, and rate facets of the message should be systematically varied in order to observe the child's performance more completely.

> The clinician can present semantic concepts from the child's classroom materials in increasingly complex syntactic constructions, with and without contextual cues, with a normal speaking rate and with a slowed rate. Observe any breakdown in performance or improvement in performance by varying these factors (Lasky and Chapandy 1976, p. 167).

All of these receptive considerations have a direct bearing upon the child's performance in the classroom, and the evaluation process should include observations on them. These receptive evaluation data need to be shared with the child's teacher so that modifications (such as reducing instructional speech rate or rewording complex directions) can be implemented.

Expressive Evaluation

When evaluating expressive language, both language form (structure) and function flexibility need to be observed. The clinician must bear in mind that communicative competence is not synonymous with knowledge of syntax. Communicative competence is much more comprehensive in that it focuses on language within context — and one operates in *varying* contexts. To be stated in another way:

> Speaking and understanding language always takes place in context. We know our mother tongue in the sense of *using* it — not as an abstract system of vocal signals. We know it in the sense of knowing how to use it; we know how to communicate with our people, how to choose forms of language that are appropriate to the type of situation we find ourselves in (Halliday 1978, p. 13).

The functional view of language, to which this author adheres, is interested in what the speaker can *do* with language. "Learning to speak is mastery of a behavior potential" (Halliday 1978).

Language Sample

By beginning with a gross measure, such as a language sample, it is possible to individualize the evaluation procedure. You begin with a situation that allows you to observe what the individual *does* with language informally and under specific demands (such as describing a sequential picture story, making up a story, instructing you on how to make a phone call, or explaining how various components of a bicycle interact to make it move).

It is possible to tap message effectiveness at various levels of language development. For example, if it is observed that the child is speaking in only two- to three-word units, the clinician can draw upon the evaluation model proposed by MacDonald and Blott (1974) and MacDonald (1978). Effectiveness would be measured in terms of how many of the eight semantic–grammatical rules (see Appendix 2) are being used by the child. For the more advanced child, the clinician could use an applied transformational model (Hannah 1978) combined with an applied use of Halliday's (1973) model that describes the seven basic functions of child language (see page 34). In other words, the goal would be to evaluate how well the child chooses appropriate forms of language and knows how to use them for various speech acts (to describe, inquire, interact socially, hypothesize, and so on). It is the author's opinion that for the clinician to realize the optimum value of a language sample, this procedure cannot be totally unstructured. (See Appendices 4 through 9 and Section IV for specific suggestions on how the clinician can provide opportunities for the child to *use* language for various purposes and then observe his facility in doing so.)

In addition to sampling the child's spontaneous language, it is important to probe for a possible gap between his performance and his competence. Morehead and Johnson (1972) found that language–deficient children frequently do not habitually use the language knowledge that they really *do* possess. Their research indicated that these children demonstrate constraints on the underlying rule systems that they do possess. This, they inferred, probably reflects restricted creativity in the use of their rule system during language production. To evaluate this possible gap between performance and competence, the author asks a child to look at a set of sequential pictures and to tell the story. When the child has finished, the author then says, "That was great. I have a story about these pictures, too. I want you to listen to my story very carefully. When I'm finished, I want you to tell me *my* story about the pictures." (With children approximately five to ten years of age, it is referred to as playing "Copy Cat.") The task of perceiving relevant relationships within the pictorial story and creating constructions that map these relationships has been simplified for the child. The clinician is now in the position of comparing the two versions of the story to see if more details, more relationships, and more complex syntax appear. In other words, the clinician wants to find out if it is possible to remove constraints and to *prime* abilities that are present but that are not being used. (Appendix 6 presents an example of this competence/performance gap.)

Correlate Tests

Whatever information the clinician has not been able to acquire during a language sample should be sought through the judicious use of formal or informal (Leonard, Prutting, Perozzi and Berkley 1978) correlate tests. The tests chosen should be determined by the presenting behaviors of the individual being evaluated. For example, if a particular child showed only irregular verb syntactic errors in his language sample, it would be a waste of time to present him with the *Northwestern Syntax Screening Test* (Lee 1969) as a matter of testing routine. It would, however, be worthwhile to investigate how many irregular verbs he did not know (an informal measure) as well as how many other nonredundant features of the language he did not know. The latter could be quickly screened through the use of the Grammatic Closure Subtest (a formal measure) of the *Illinois Test of Psycholinguistics* (Kirk, McCarthy and Kirk 1968).

Noting the child's score on a test should only be the initial step in observing test performance. Error analysis is the basis of description upon which remediation programs can be formulated.

When administering and scoring standardized tests, the manual procedures must be consulted and followed. Once an objective score has been ascertained, however, there is no reason that the clinician cannot engage in some "creative manipulation" of the testing situation. For example, the justification process used in Piaget's *method clinique* (Sigel and Cocking 1977) can reveal some interesting information on the child's problem–solving style. Secondly, clinician–devised scoring procedures can be developed. For example, while the clinician might not want to use the percentile descriptions of the *Northwestern Syntax Screening Test* (Lee 1969), it is useful to note (1) which types of sentences are missed on the receptive versus the expressive sections, (2) how these performances compare with the data extracted from the sample (Prutting, Gallagher and Mulac 1975), and (3) the percentage of items answered correctly on each section during the baseline administration as contrasted to performance after therapy.

All evaluation data can be summarized so that a longitudinal record of performance is available (see Appendix 10). In a quick glance one can observe gains the student has made.

The single guideline for selecting correlate tests should be to supplement clinician knowledge about the child's language proficiency to the degree that something will be done about it. If certain test results will just gather dust or will fail to provide *additional* information, then the test should not be used.

Muma (1973) discusses a number of important procedural considerations for gathering descriptive, representative data during an evaluation that demonstrate the underlying rules responsible for the child's dysfunctional communication.

As Siegel and Broen (1976) pointed out, the evaluation process should reflect the clinician's conception of language function and dysfunction. This conception is dynamic; it is innervated by new knowledge that becomes available to the clinician through research and clinical observations. One should never become slavishly attached to a static model of language that someone else has developed or cling to one's own model as if it were a sacred revelation.

Teacher Referrals

Arrange to speak at the initial faculty meeting held at your school in the fall. Provide a description of expressive and receptive communicative competence and incompetence.

Make available Loban's Oral Language Scale (Appendix 11) as a referral checklist. Encourage teachers to refer children who would tend to score in the 4 to 5 range on the Oral Language Scale. In addition, provide some descriptive guidelines for competent and incompetent receptive language so that students with language processing problems will also be referred. These language processing guidelines can be extracted from Wiig and Semel (1976).

To summarize Premise I, it is the clinician's responsibility to develop a dynamic conceptual model of communicative competence and then to evaluate an individual's communicative effectiveness in terms of its congruence with or divergence from communicative competence. Observations are gathered through representative sampling of the individual's expressive language and through a selective use of correlate tests. It is the description of the discrepancy between the conceptual model of competence and the current level of student functioning that leads directly to programming goals.

PREMISE II

Evaluative data need to be organized for clinician analysis. The integrity of each linguistic component (phonology, morphology, syntax, and semantics) and interpersonal communication (coherent exchange of information) should be studied. Individualized Educational Plans (IEPs) should be constructed that enable programming to begin at the point of developmental disruption and continue sequentially to the point of competence.

Sample Analysis

Evaluation establishes a baseline by describing the child's current communication skills. Through analysis of evaluation data, the clinician can organize a sequential remediation program to develop deficient skills. These sequential program components can be stated in terms of short–term objectives on the child's IEP.

In analyzing the sample transcription, the clinician should note what the child *does* have in grammatical knowledge (Hannah 1977) and what the child does *not* have (Tyack and Gottsleben 1974). In other words, constructions relied upon and patterns of errors should be determined. Hannah (1977) has developed a Linguistic Development Summary Sheet (Appendix 7) that lists the most common basal constructions and transformations. This form can be used to record the constructions relied upon by the child. Tyack and Gottsleben (1974) concentrate on the percentage of obligatory contexts in which a construction appears, thus determining the error patterns of the child. For example, when surveying a transcription, the clinician might note that the child is omitting auxiliary "is" much of the time. The next step would be to determine how much of the time. This is accomplished by observing all obligatory contexts (for use of auxiliary "is") and calculating a percentage of occurrence versus nonoccurrence of the structure. This provides a base for therapy accountability. If the structure was omitted 68 percent of the time when the child was originally evaluated but only 39 percent of the time after six weeks of therapy, then there is some evidence of learning. It can be discouraging to work with a child for six weeks and ponder, "He is *still* omitting auxiliary 'is.' " When the baseline figure (68 percent) is compared with the later error rate (39 percent), however, it becomes obvious that some progress has been achieved. A brief example of the author's approach to sample notation of error patterns appears as Appendix 5 and an example of a language sample scenario, transcription and analysis appears as Appendix 9.

Brown's (1973) data indicate that while there is a correlation of .68 between age and linguistic development, there is a .92 correlation between MLU and linguistic development. Lee (1969) points out that sentence length becomes less important when evaluating language development than the transformational complexity of the surface structure. She goes on to explain:

The thirteen-word sentence, "The dog is sitting on a chair in the corner of the room," is not a difficult sentence to comprehend nor to compose. It is a kernel sentence with subject and verb in actor-action sequence. One could even guess the meaning, without resorting to grammatical structure at all, just by knowing the contentives: dog, sit, chair, corner, room. But the shorter eight-word sentence, "Why didn't she want him to sit down?" is a highly transformed sentence, much more difficult to comprehend or to compose (Lee 1969, p. 273).

It is this author's experience that MLU is a worthwhile *general* notation to calculate, along with notations on the degree of complexity that characterizes sentence formation. For example, it is recommended that the clinician note:

1. Relative percentages of:
   a. sentence fragments.
   b. simple sentences.
   c. expanded sentences (with prepositional phrases).
   d. compound sentences (two simple sentences joined with a conjunction).
   e. complex sentences (one sentence embedded within another).
   f. sentences showing combinations of expansion, conjunction and embedding.

2. Word versus morpheme counts for MLUs of 5.0 and below, because it comments on the child's use of inflections ("He go to the store" — five words; "He goes to the store" — six morphemes).

These notations, along with those of Hannah's (1977) Linguistic Developmental Summary Sheet (see Appendix 7), provide a useful description of the types of constructions upon which the child is relying.

Organization of Evaluation Data

All descriptive information (from the language sample and correlate tests) should be organized on the Clinician Worksheet (Appendix 8). This permits the clinician to summarize the integrity of each linguistic component as well as that of interpersonal communication. The author has found it clinically efficient to separate syntactic from morphological problems on the Clinicial Worksheet, with the latter referring only to the child's use of inflections. The semantic value of words is focused upon, and therefore vocabulary notations are made under the "semantics" category on the Worksheet. This organization is crucial to comprehensive programming. Without this step, it is likely that some aspects of necessary programming will be overlooked. (See Appendix 4 for a summary of evaluation and analytical procedures suggested in Premises I and II.)

Writing IEPs

Only when the clinician has gathered and organized the descriptive data on language form and function can productive IEPs be formulated. By consulting the Clinician Worksheet, it becomes apparent which communication skills the child needs to develop. If the needs are then sequenced developmentally, the short-term objectives are automatically delineated (see Appendix 12). As developmentally sequenced short-term objectives are met, they can be checked off, and the clinician can proceed down the list until deficiencies in each area have been remediated to criterion level. The purpose of IEPs is to systematically remediate deficient skills; it is important to remember this *raison d' etre* of IEPs and not to let unnecessary paper work (or evaluation) detract from therapy time.

Long-term language structure objectives can be stated in terms of the percentage of restricted versus nonrestricted sentences in a fifty-sentence sample (Hannah 1977) that should be expected by the end of the academic year. (A restricted sentence is one in which a grammatical error is present.) For the more involved cases (where there are multiple restrictions *per sentence*), the number of restricted forms per sentence can be stated. Let's look at an example of each.

Percentage of Restrictions Per Sample

Let's say a child showed 57 percent restricted sentences in the spring of first grade. When the clinician would write his IEP for the following year, it might read, "By May 30, 1979 (the end of second grade), John will show no more than 45 percent restricted sentences within a fifty–sentence language sample." In other words, by using the prior sample as a baseline, the clinician can formulate a "ball park" figure that satisfies administrative needs for accountability stated in numerical terms, and yet that offers great flexibility in programming planning not possible through statement of score advances on particular tests. The author has found that a 10 to 15 percent reduction in restricted sentences per year is a cautious estimate. Such a statement covers all short–term objectives for remediation of problems in the areas of morphology and syntax. Semantic problems (such as word choice errors or lack of meaningful relationships among words or phrases within a sentence) may be considered separately or included as one of the factors that is restricting the sentence.

Number of Restricted Forms Per Sentence

Once again, let's look at a hypothetical case. Sue showed 3.5 restrictions *per sentence* in the spring of 1978. Her long–term objective might read, "By May 30, 1979, Sue will show an average of no more than 2.0 restrictions per sentence within a fifty–sentence language sample." This type of objective would be appropriate for a child whose sample showed 80 to 100 percent restricted sentences. Obviously, for these more severe syntax–deviant cases, the scope of the long–term objective has to be reduced. To increase this individual's communicative competence, the first step would be a preliminary one: since the vast majority of sentences show restrictions and since each sentence shows multiple restrictions, reduction of the *degree* of restriction per sentence needs to precede an objective to reduce the number of restricted sentences within a sample.

It is emphasized that functional advances are of equal importance to structural advances. Notation, therefore, should be made either within a dual form–function long–term objective, indicating the number of language functions in which the clinician expects the child to show appropriate age–proficiency. For example (in a *dual* form–function objective), "By May 30, 1979, Mark will show no more than 45 percent restricted sentences within a fifty–sentence language sample *and* will show proficiency within the clinic, as judged by the clinician, in the instrumental and interactional functions of language."

Obviously, children who have phonological problems will need an appropriate objective appended to the long–term objective, or a separate long–term objective, to cover remediation of these deficient linguistic skills. An example of an objective for a phonological problem might be, "By May 30, 1979, Jim will be able to produce initial /r/ in monosyllabic words at his normal speech speed with 90 percent accuracy as judged by the clinician."

Examples of IEP short–term objectives are provided in Appendix 13.

End of the Year IEP Review

It cannot be assumed that because a child has met an IEP objective in October, the behavior has completely stabilized. Therefore, it is recommended that as part of the end–of–year evaluation, IEP objectives be reviewed. If a child has reached 100 percent accuracy using auxiliary *is/was* in sequential stories and an earlier objective was use of auxiliary *is/was* in drill, it is not necessary to automatically review auxiliary *is/was* in drill. If, however, when auxiliary *is/was* is reviewed in sequential stories and the child shows only 60 percent accuracy, then you should review performance at the drill level. In other words, first review performance at its highest level of attainment and if there is less than 80 percent accuracy, then review earlier objectives that were precursors to the higher performance level. (See Appendix 14 for an example of an IEP Review Checklist.) These data will help to establish IEP priorities for the ensuing fall semester. Any behavior that has not stabilized needs to be included in the first short–term objectives written for September.

Ineffectiveness of Diagnostic Labels

The purpose of evaluation and individualized programming is to ensure that a certain remediation strategy is not arbitrarily used with all children, nor that all "mentally retarded" children do not automatically receive the same instructional approach. Programming should always be unique to the individual and not based on some diagnostic label, such as "autistic," "aphasic," or "mentally retarded." As Rosenthal, Eisenson and Luckau (1972) emphasized, diagnostic labels are inefficient and frequently counterproductive. From their data, compiled from two separate research studies, these authors concluded that classification of disorders is of little importance unless that system of classification segregates children with respect to treatment options. To paraphrase Swisher (1975), who succinctly described how to play the "label game" if the clinician is confronted with it:

> You look around at the educational opportunities available for children with special problems. You visit the facilities and note the types of developmental programming that each facility and room therein offers and you ask the program administrator how each of these groupings is labeled. After you assess a child's needs, you put the label on him which will allow him to be admitted into the most appropriate program.

The IEP can become the clinician's best monitor of systematic programming that has been individualized to the unique needs of a unique child, thus transforming an administrative necessity into an aid to clinical efficiency rather than a deterrent.

To summarize Premise II, organization of evaluation data should precede any attempt to establish developmental programs; the *comprehensive* needs of the individual should be considered. Long-term and short–term IEP objectives can be constructed from the list of deficits in each area on the Clinician Worksheet. Check off each objective as the child reaches the criterion level and then proceed down the list until you have programmed for every deficit skill noted.

PREMISE III

Therapy methodology should reflect the diversity of skills needed within one's case load. Increased communication proficiency is intrinsically motivating and reinforcing. Realistic increments can be gradually achieved through task analysis and developmental programming.

Clinician Versatility in Programming

The human being by nature has ideas, feelings, needs and perceptions and wants to communicate them. If a child has not "cracked the code" during the linguistically formative years or learned to use language effectively in a variety of contexts, then learning strategies need to be created which will help him to successfully approximate proficient communication through realistically incremental steps.

This premise addresses itself in particular to the consideration of the *types* of proficiency that might need to be nurtured within any one caseload. Once again, the focus is directed to considering the way in which any one individual might not meet the *comprehensive* criteria of "communicative competence."

There was a time when the speech–language clinician was considered a "speech correctionist." A screening of school children consisted of noting whether or not a child could produce the "speech sounds" in the language. Therapy methodology consisted of "ear training" initially and later playing games that just happened to require the child to say "his sound" periodically. If one were to consider the Clinician Worksheet (Appendix 8) as a reference, it would become apparent that if a clinician's methodology consisted of only articulation development strategies, methodologies to serve the other four areas would be absent.

We have become aware of the fact that communicative competence is a lot more than "saying the speech sounds correctly." In addition, we have become aware of varying types of methodologies available to service the divergent communication needs. It is important to match the methodology with the type of communication need as well as to use it at the optimal time in the therapy sequence. (An example of this sequencing is provided on pages 13 and 14.)

Five different types of cases are offered next for the purpose of emphasizing the versatility and diversity needed in a clinician's "bag of tricks." This is by no means an attempt to *label* the cases; it is an attempt to describe the diversity one may expect in a caseload and therefore need to develop appropriate methodologies to meet varying needs.

Depending upon a facility's structure of educational management and the geographical region, a clinician could have at least five different types of language cases for whom programming would be necessary:

1. the nearly nonverbal or emerging language case;
2. the child who is in the process of cracking the structural (syntactic and morphological) code;
3. the marginal communicator;
4. the language–different child; and
5. the child whose primary difficulty is intelligibility.

Obviously, the clinicians's goals for developing communicative competence vary not only among these categories, but for each child who falls primarily within one of the categories as contrasted to the others. Once again, the categories are not intended as diagnostic labels, but rather are offered for purposes of caseload description.

Five Types of Language Cases

1. Emerging Language

Our earlier discussion of the hypothetical child and the sequencing of theoretical and empirical data to meet his programming needs (pages 11 through 14) provided an example of the first category of cases, "emerging language." In addition to the sequential development outlined earlier, it is crucial for this type of case in particular that the clinican consider himself an "environmental engineer." During any contact with the child, the clinician should use the context for developing a better understanding of the linguistic system. For example, if the clinician plans an activity such as drawing and asks the child to comment on what he is doing, capitalize on the moment the child accidentally drops the crayon:

Clinician: Oh – drop crayon. What happened?
Child: Drop crayon.
Clinician: Crayon is on the floor. Crayon floor. Where is crayon?

```
Child:      Crayon floor.
Clinician:  Pick up the crayon. Brian get crayon. What did you do?
Child:      Brian get crayon.
```

Another example of capitalizing on the moment was mentioned by Holland (1975). A student clinician was attempting to teach the cognitive–linguistic concept of "more" using the modifier/head semantic–grammatical rule. All attempts failed until the child spotted a box of Kleenex on the therapy room table. He began pulling out the pieces of Kleenex, and as the child did so, the clinician emphasized "*more* Kleenex, *more* Kleenex," and so on. Due to the clinician being an "environmental engineer," the child left the therapy session with the semantic–grammatical rule of modifier/head and the concept "more."

2. Cracking the Code

There are some children who have not learned to supply certain structural units required by English grammar. They may substitute one form for another (such as objective pronoun *her* for subjective pronoun *she*), or they may omit forms (such as functors like "the," "is," or inflections at the end of words such as *–s, –ing,* or *–ed*). They are in the process of figuring out the language system at a much later age, and frequently in an atypical sequence. Researchers generally agree that by age five or six, only a few differences between child and adult grammar are noticeable (such as refinement of subject/verb agreement, irregular past tense, and past perfect tense forms [Dale 1976]).

3. Marginal Communicators

This category of cases is composed of students whom a clinician and teacher recognize as not communicating effectively, although structural deviations neither describe some of the bizarre communicative patterns nor do they offer adequate goals for clinician intervention (Rees 1978). Although this student may have *some* structural deviations (such as a lack of a consistent tense reference in a sentence or paragraph or limited knowledge of the irregular features of English grammar), the primary problem area is interpersonal communication; there is an inordinate difficulty in coherently transferring a message composed of explicit referents from the individual's thoughts into words. A "sputtering" of information characterizes output rather than a logical development of the information. By synthesizing observations of several researchers who have studied nonproficient communication behaviors it is possible to create a rather descriptive composite of the marginal communicator's typically ineffective communication style.

Blue (1975) coined the term "marginal communicator," using it to describe the child who communicates little, and when he does venture forth, communicates ineptly. The child seems not to have developed "the necessary internal motivation to use and acquire reward from socially interactive speech" (Blue 1975, p. 33).

Rees (1978) observes that this individual cannot carry on a conversation that "maintains the flow of meaning." Steiner (1969) comments that this individual does not use language to achieve his potential either in the development of self or of a role in relation to others.

There are limitations in the flexibility of language usage. Bernstein (1964, 1970) describes these limitations in terms of the individual's reliance upon a "restricted code," as contrasted to an "elaborated code." In general, the restricted code assumes the presence of common knowledge that does not exist. It is, therefore, difficult for the listener to determine the speaker's referents. "He gave him the bag and he left," for example, contains an ambiguous referent. It is impossible for the listener to know *who* left — the person who brought the bag or the person who received it. Halliday (1973, 1978) described the restricted code as representing limited functions of language. In other words, the child is unable to shift appropriately from one contextual (or purposive) use of language to another. Both Bernstein and Halliday emphasize that the two codes (or different strategies of language use based upon the speaker's interpretations of what the situation demands) refer to performance rather than competence. Bereiter and Engelmann (1966) describe this lack of flexibility as limited practice in the "cognitive uses" of language. In other words, there is very little skill or comfort, or both, displayed in using language to describe, explain, instruct, inquire, analyze, compare/contrast, evaluate, and hypothesize.

The marginal communicator is a very intriguing case and one frequently overlooked (Blue 1975). "We can't afford to 'wait until he feels like talking' or until 'he grows out of it,' for the result is, too often, a young adult with reduced skills who fails to communicate satisfactorily with his employer and fellow workers" (Blue 1975, p. 36). The distinguishing characteristics of this type of case have been discussed in Section II and summarized on pages 38 and 39.

4. The Language-Different Child

The concept of the language-different child refers primarily to the student who speaks a dialect of English or is bilingual, and secondarily refers to the student whose cultural or socioeconomic background is sufficiently different from that of the educators and their expectations that the student appears linguistically deviant.

This is a difficult case to discuss. There are two biases that need to be stated:

1. This student should not be treated as "language-disordered."
2. Both form and function differences need to be considered.

Leonard (1972) touched upon a delineation among delay, disorder and difference:

1. *Language delay* involves correct sequence, but delay in emergence.
2. *Language disorder* involves disruption in time and sequence of emergence.
3. *Language difference* involves linguistic interference.

This delineation serves the purpose of separating deviances in *form* among these populations. Halliday (1978) helps to complete the description of language difference. "The teacher, subject matter and the system are the factors that tend to put the language different child at a disadvantage and raise the odds against him. It is not a linguistic disadvantage but a social disadvantage. . . . Linguistic remedies [alone] are not the answer" (Halliday 1978, p. 104). We will take time to consider both the form and function differences of this student so that programming justifications for him can be better understood.

If these children are not considered "disordered," what might the clinician's role be in programming for them? The author suggests (1) contrastive analysis, and (2) expansion of language functions.

Contrastive Analysis. Just as researchers have established that the speech of a child is not a *random* deviation from adult norms, so speech analysis of culturally diverse groups has demonstrated that these linguistic systems are in conformity with their own sets of rules. Analytical research is available from numerous sources on Black dialect, including Labov and Cohen (1966), Fasold and Wolfram (1974), and Williams (1970). Research on Spanish/English bilingualism is described in a variety of works, including Dulay and Burt (1973), O'Brien (1973), and Dulay, Hernandez-Chavez and Burt (1978). In addition, there is a monograph available through the American Speech and Hearing Association prepared by Williams and Wolfram (1977) that discusses five social dialects in the United States. The author mentions these resources to emphasize that if the clinician is to differentiate between language disorder and language difference, an attempt must be made to understand predictable deviations from standard English when a child is filtering his communication through a dialect of English or a different linguistic system.

The clinician is encouraged to become acquainted with predictable deviations. Language samples should be analyzed in terms of utterances that show disorder (those deviations that could not be predicted) versus difference (those deviations that could be predicted).

In "contrastive analysis" (or bi–dialectal programming), a consciousness is developed regarding the difference between "book–talk" and "talk–talk." "Book–talk" refers to normal, standard English that is used in textbooks and "talk–talk" is the child's vernacular (Gerber, Francis and Ecroyd 1973). While there is no attempt to teach the language–different child to *speak* standard English, an awareness of it as an alternative mode of expression is developed. Difference is viewed, then, as "nonstandard" rather than "substandard" (Williams 1970).

As Adler (1971) has pointed out, we are a pluralistic society of numerous subcultures arising from ethnic and class distinctions and linguistic and behavioral differences. Differences should be encouraged, but as Adler suggests, a bi–dialectal program (or contrastive analysis) can help develop communicative flexibility. In those situations where the individual is expected to switch to a more formal code, he will be able to do so. Language flexibility is related to the degree of academic success and socioeconomic mobility one may enjoy.

Two contexts, for example, in which the individual might be expected to switch to a more formal code are in theme composition and completing an application form for an employer who is outside the individual's cultural milieu. Sometimes the meaning of written work might be unclear to teachers or future employers when stated in the rules of a different linguistic system. In addition, the employer might want evidence that the individual could compose written communication in standard English for company correspondence. The individual should have the resources to shift to a more neutral (or standard) code when the context necessitates it.

An additional consideration is the indication that while language–different students do not have excessive reading comprehension difficulties in the primary grades, problems do begin to surface around third grade (Moore 1971). As Moore (1971) and Lasky and Chapandy (1976) have pointed out, from third grade onward, texts focus on content, with increasingly complex semantics and syntax. In other words, instead of purposely reducing the rigors of the subject matter so that attention can be directed to developing decoding skills (as is done in the first two grades), textbooks and teachers assume that the child is comfortable with adult, standard English language structure as well as with basic reading skills and can now proceed with the real thrust of education — to question and explore knowledge. A firm base in "textbook English" at an analytical level is an asset when semantic and syntactic complexity begin to interact in the middle grades. This assumption is based on research findings on the relationships between reading success and the ability to make use of all phonemic, morphological, and syntactic cues (Wiig and Semel 1976).

Contrastive analysis (or developing an awareness between "talk–talk" and "book–talk") is an "Expose — Don't Impose" philosophy (O'Brien 1973). The child is introduced to an alternate (school textbook) code, but is not penalized nor embarrassed for speaking a dialect. In the author's clinical experience, students seem most responsive to contrastive analysis from approximately age ten.

Functional Expansion. A child spends approximately five exclusive, formative years within his home and community environments. Educators assume that these years have provided growth opportunities for the basic language uses that are relied upon within the school setting. If, because of different cultural or sociolinguistic interactive styles, this is not the case, then the child appears at a disadvantage. It is not being suggested that the child might have come from a "culturally deprived" or "culturally disadvantaged" background; it is being suggested that if he comes from a culturally *different* background he might not have the expanded functions of language upon which the school relies for the transmission of knowledge. Halliday (1978) comments that Bernstein has identified the regulative, instructional, imaginative and interpersonal functions of language as being critical in the child's linguistic socialization. Let's examine more closely some of the assumptions about homogeniety of student language skills made by educators and some of the different interactional patterns that might develop in culturally diverse (nonstandard, working class) family social systems that tend to be "at odds" with the educational social system.

    a. *Expectations.* The teacher operates on the assumption that by the time the child arrives in school, language as a means of learning has been established. For example, it is assumed that language as a means of personal expression and participation is ready to be *extended* to a new context, school (Halliday 1978). In addition, it is expected that if the child does not understand something, he will ask questions.

    b. *Culturally diverse patterns.* People develop a comfortable communication mode with a range of variants. Some modes and their variants have more prestige than others in a hierarchical social structure (Halliday 1978). To be more specific,

> large numbers of city children learn to speak (or learn to mean) in ways which are incompatible with established social norms. This would not matter if these norms were not embodied in the principles and practices of education (Halliday 1978, p. 186).

> Obviously, we need not single out only "city children." We are focusing on any group of children whose "mode and variants" are different from those valued within the school setting.

Bernstein's research (1962, 1964, 1967, 1970) has investigated the variables within the home and cultural environment of the child that affect his attitudes toward communication with adults in school as well as developing a certain specificity in expression that is essential when manipulating language for reasoning tasks, or other context–free uses. While the restricted versus the elaborated code has been discussed earlier (pages 27 through 29), the focus here is on the effects of culture on language functions.

Social Structure and Language Development. Generally, Bernstein states that language is controlled by social structure and that the social structure is maintained and transmitted through language (Halliday 1978). It is essential to the interpretation of Bernstein's theoretical and empirical works that language be thought of as *meaning* rather than structure; it is a functional view of language: how well does the individual's communication style serve his needs in varying contexts? A relationship exists between social roles learned and communication style used.

Bernstein (1970) notes four basic socializing systems (family, peer group, school, and work) and that within each system, the individual occupies certain roles. First, the child is a member of a family system and engages in its role relationships and the typical communication patterns derived from these role relationships, and then gradually he participates in the other systems. The nature of the socializing system somewhat determines the range of behavioral opportunities available to the child and, consequently, the different types of communication opportunities that occur. In other words, critical socializing contexts may lead to changes in language learning strategies and, hence, changes in the meaning potential that is typically associated with various environments.

> What Bernstein's work suggests is that there may be differences in the relative orientation of different social groups towards the various functions of language in given contexts and towards the different areas of meaning that may be explored *within* a given function. . . . Suppose that the functions that are relatively stressed by one group are positive with respect to school. They are favored and extended in the educational process, while those that are relatively stressed by another group are largely irrelevant or even negative in the educational context. We have, then, a plausible interpretation of the role of language in educational failure (Halliday 1978, p. 106).

It should be quite evident that Bernstein's theory is a difference, not a deficit, theory—differences of interpretation of experience, evaluation, and orientation.

Let's look at one facet of the family socializing system that tends to develop communication styles that are either consonant or dissonant with the expectations of school: the closed versus the open social system. Bernstein (1970) says that in a closed social system, there is a position-oriented attitude prevalent, while an open social system tends to be person-oriented. Position- versus person-oriented family role systems can be determined by how decision-making is approached (i.e., the extent and kinds of interactions that occur among family members).

In position-oriented systems there is a formal division of rights and responsibilities according to age, sex, and position. For example, the child's communication system might be open only in relation to peers, and they would become the major source of learning and relevance. The child gets meager person-to-person interaction with adults. In addition, there is generally a weak or closed communication system in position-oriented families. This type of family does not encourage the verbal exploration of individual intentions and motives. The child responds to status requirements; he learns the communalized role as distinct from the individualized role stressed in person-oriented families. As such, there are far fewer opportunities for practicing language as a means of personal expression and participation. A position-oriented family is likely to establish prescribed role behaviors for each family member, thus creating an atmosphere where there is a smaller range of alternative behaviors for each family member. For example, should Grandfather state, "Children are to be seen and not heard," it would be treated as a law — not a debatable philosophical precept. The opportunity for dialogue, in which two points of view are articulated, logically supported, and dissected would rarely occur.

> The greater the range of alternatives permitted by the role system, the more individualized the verbal meanings, the higher the order [of thinking] and the more flexible the syntactic and vocabulary selection and so the more elaborated the code (Bernstein 1970, p. 34).

By contrast, says Bernstein, a family type where the range of decisions, modifications, and judgments are a function of the psychological qualities of the person, there is a person-oriented decision-making milieu. Here there is a range of alternatives of the role in different social situations. Judgments and their bases and consequences occupy a major place in communications. The role system is continuously accommodating and assimilating the different intents of its members; children end up socializing parents as much as parents socialize the children because the parents are sensitive to the unique characteristics of their child. Individual differences are verbally expressed and reinforced. A role system of this kind promotes communication and orientation toward the motives and dispositions of others. "Children socialized within such a role and communication system learn to cope with ambiguity and ambivalence" (Bernstein 1970, p. 39). Obviously, such family-role preparation is very healthy in the educational environment; education is inquiry *because* so much of our universe is steeped in ambiguity and ambivalence. "To wonder is to begin to understand."

Moore (1971) indicated that the socioeconomic status of the language-different child is more of a determiner of his school communicative success than his dialect. Moore's review of sociolinguistic research showed that working-class children, for example, seem reluctant to take the verbal initiative with adults and frequently are even instructed by their mothers to be passive in school. "Fragmentary evidence suggests that the lower-class child enters school with a hesitancy to question, to initiate verbal interactions with adults and, in general, to gain important information through verbal means" (Moore 1971, p. 26). This might be attributed to a factor noted by Bernstein (1967) that the working-class mother tends to be status- rather than person-oriented in her verbal communications with her child, while the middle-class mother is more oriented to the personal development of her child's intellect.

Degree of Linguistic Specificity. Rees (1978) cited a study by Parisi and Gianelli that corroborated an observation made by Bernstein that middle-class children use considerably more nouns in their descriptions than do working-class children. Parisi and Gianelli suggested that between 1½ and 2½ years of age, middle-class children have already begun to depend less upon the context to carry their meanings. Since noun phrases are easily substituted with pronouns *in context,* working-class children rely more on the context to "spell out" the noun phrase, and hence they develop less extensive noun vocabularies.

Language Differences and the Educational System. Educational resistance can result from the child's discomfort with the mode and variations of the social system embodied in education. The child's discomfort arises from the difference in the ways in which social reality has been developed within his home and community and those styles that are dominant in schools and instructional materials. It is a question of how "culturally mainstreamed" the child has been prior to his school entrance.

Who should adapt to whom? While Bereiter and Engelmann (1966) stress that the child must change to meet the expectations of the prolonged socializing system of school, Ginsburg (1972) emphasizes that it is the school that must change to capitalize upon the culture and experiences the child brings with him to school. Bernstein (1970) and Halliday (1978) take a moderate view, as does the author. "Educational institutions are faced with the problems of encouraging children to extend the way they use language" (Bernstein 1970, p. 50).

The ideal would be for the schools to reflect the multi-cultural society; this is unlikely, however. A twofold compromise is recommended:

1. to accept the child's vernacular (dialect system) for oral language, but request standard English for written work, and

2. to help the child expand language functions that are valued in "the Establishment."

"We do not have to teach children [to speak] formal grammar in order for them to use an elaborated code. There is nothing, but nothing, in a dialect as such, which prevents a child from internalizing and learning to use universalistic meaning" (Bernstein 1970, p. 57).

Responsibility for change should not be left solely to the child; attention should not be diverted from conditions and contexts of learning in school that also need to develop more flexibility. Moore (1971) offers suggestions, from his synthesis of research on culturally diverse children, for a "compensatory program" (Appendix 15). Bernstein's criticism of the compensatory education concept described by Bereiter and Engelmann (1966) is that it focuses upon deficiencies within the community, family, and the child and distracts attention from the deficiencies in the school. "If the culture of the middle-class teacher is to become part of the consciousness of the child, then the culture of the child must first be in the consciousness of the teacher. . . . We should start to realize that the social experience the child already possesses is valid and significant" (Bernstein 1970, pp. 57–58). As O'Brien (1973, p. 21) advises, "Language is part of the culture and culture is integral to the self-concept, so we must work with cultural-linguistic differences."

There is no such thing as homogeneity when it comes to language cases; that is why labels are so ineffective and inefficient. We cannot say, "Ah, a language-different child — a compensatory program is necessary." It is not the intent of the author to imply that *all* language-different children come from "position-oriented" family social systems, or that all children who come from "poisition-oriented" family social systems are language-different. The observations of sociolinguists have been shared so that clinicians can better understand how cultural differences *might* produce differences in communication experiences and communication styles.

5. Intelligibility Cases

There are two subclassifications of intelligibility cases: (1) articulation–based, and (2) style–based.

Articulation–Based. For some children it becomes a monumental task to learn where to put the tongue in order to produce English phonemes. In some cases it is a question of exchanging one bundle of distinctive phoneme features for another (Pollack and Rees 1972), and in other cases it might be a pattern of behavior that is more pervasive than the simple substitution of one set of features for another. Panagos (1974), for example, discusses the "open syllable" syndrome that some children exhibit and views it as a language disorder rather than an articulation disorder; the child has not learned the linguistic rule that words have final sounds. (He elaborates on this basic observation and the interested reader is directed to his article for more specific information.)

Programming for articulation–based cases should focus on the "overlapping, ballistic movements" of speech (McDonald 1964) and the achievement of accuracy of production at speech speed (Gerber 1973). Drill at the syllable level, therefore, is efficient because it concentrates on the problem sound within the rigors of overlapping sounds at a normal speech rate. Like any motor behavior, articulation development should proceed within a framework of repetition. Every minute of the therapy session should be an opportunity to practice production. Mowrer (1970) discussed the futility of ridiculous speech games that direct the child's attention away from the task at hand (i.e., increasing his motor control over speech sounds). Attention to the number of responses per minute allows the therapist to objectively evaluate whether or not the therapy session has been an efficient use of time.

Style–Based. The second type of intelligibility case is actually not a true "articulation" case. Speech is characterized by a gliding from one word to another so that the speech sounds slurred and sloppy. Bereiter and Engelmann (1966) have described this behavior as "the giant word syndrome." Many words are elided; unless the listener has the benefit of strong contextual clues, it is a strain to decipher the speaker's semantic intent. For example, "My father gave me some," might sound like "M–far–game–sa." (See Section IV, example 8.) For some children, the etiology for such production might be neurological; for others, it is a habit. For neurologically involved cases, absolutely clear speech frequently needs to be abandoned as a goal and a compensatory style of speaking developed. Such a style would stress a speech speed that allows the individual's articulators sufficient time to move from one phoneme to the next. This might mean, for example, reducing speech rate from 90 words per minute down to 60 words per minute. Additionally, an awareness of the listener's need for intelligiblity should be developed; this presents a rationale for reducing the speech rate. The approach with those who seemingly have no neurological reason for this speech style does not really differ. The clinician might comment, "I cannot understand you. I think that you are making yourself talk too fast. We need to find a speech speed that is more comfortable for you so that listeners can understand your words. You have a lot of important things to say. People want to understand you!" Keep in mind that speech is part of the total being. If a person moves slowly and reacts slowly, there is no reason for him (or his listeners) to expect his speech to acquire "supersonic" momentum. It has been the author's observation that for some of these individuals who have acquired sloppy speech habits, it seems to represent an attempt to keep pace verbally with a fast-moving and fast-talking world. People become impatient when it takes someone a long time "to get it out." There develops a pressure to increase speech rate to minimize the risk of being interrupted. For other cases, especially the neurologically involved, the speed of thoughts is much greater than the neurological support system can cope with in terms of motor coordination. In either case, it seems imperative for the individual to become aware of his own neuromotor limitations, discover his optimal rate (to ensure *intelligible* speech) and then learn to incorporate this into his self-concept. Whether the etiology is neurological or habitual, consciousness about the listener's need to understand *words* should be emphasized.

Making Communication More Functional

To summarize Premise III, the speech–language clinician's programming strategies should show a versatility that reflects a comprehensive view of communicative competence. Each therapy task must be analyzed in terms of the child's baseline behavior, the goal, and the intermediate steps, so that communication skills become increasingly *functional*. To reiterate, if a child can only use two words, those two words should be based on semantic–grammatical rules that enable him to functionally manipulate his environment. If he is not incorporating the grammatical rules of the system, these need not be sequenced developmentally (Lee 1974) so that questions and statements function effectively by relating his communicative intent. Again, it is emphasized that the clinician should not stop with just structural considerations. The functions of language — instrumental, regulatory, interactional, personal, heuristic, imaginative and informational (or representational) (Halliday 1973) — vary with the communication setting and the individual's role within that setting. The child should learn to shift flexibly from one use of language to another. Stylistic concerns, such as coherence and fluency (Loban 1961), appropriate speech rate, and quality of referential skills (Glucksberg and Krauss 1967) are intrinsic to the effectiveness of each of the seven basic child language functions.

When advancement is planned in incremental steps that are motivating rather than frustrating, it is not necessary to engage in elaborate reinforcement procedures or contrived games. The fact that communication is becoming more productive and comfortable is intrinsically rewarding.

PREMISE IV

Before new communication skills can become stabilized and generalized (or "carried over"), utterances must be unlaboriously produced in a variety of drill and meaningful situations.

Speed With Accuracy

The goal of therapy is carryover of learned behaviors into spontaneous situations. Gerber (1973) insists that until communication skills learned in a therapy setting can occur unlaboriously at conversational speed, they will not be stabilized and, hence, not carried over into everyday contexts. They will remain at a "studied" level unless a "speed with accuracy" (Gerber 1973) stage of therapy is instituted. (A perspective on "speed" should always be maintained; the goal is for the new verbal behavior to be integrated into the child's natural rate of speech.) Although Gerber's book was directed toward articulation programming, her theoretical premise is just as relevant for morphological and syntactic types of therapy. If a child completes /r/ therapy saying "grrrreat," he has a terrific imitation of Tony the Tiger, but he has not stabilized /r/. If he is working on the possessive marker and says "Roger'sss coat," it is not stabilized. If he is working on auxiliary "is" and says "He IS running," the auxiliary form is not stabilized. In addition, the author has found this therapy step effective in teaching vocabulary (through picture labeling). The child is much more likely to use a word if he has learned to retrieve it *rapidly*. Otherwise, "thing" or "stuff" is frequently substituted. For any of these tasks, the clinician needs to say "Now we are going to play a beat-the-clock game. See how many of these (stimulus items) you can *correctly* tell me by the time the "blue hand" (second hand — whatever color it happens to be) gets to the 12." Gerber (1973) presents a series of "speed with accuracy" exercises for articulation development.

Stabilization of new learning can also be encouraged by asking the child to tell a flannel board story or relate an event at school. Tape record these and have the child help monitor the percentage of times a structure occurs in the obligatory contexts.

Brown (1973) proposed that we take as a criterion of mastery the child's use of the structure in 90 percent of the obligatory contexts.

Considering Communicative Contexts

A clinician's therapy strategies should have depth as well as breadth. While the emphasis in Premise III was on the breadth of strategies needed, the emphasis in Premise IV is on the depth of strategies needed to ensure that effective communication is generalized outside the clinic to many different contexts.

As Rees (1978) has pointed out, while the development of techniques and strategies for measuring and training syntax has been of significance in the advancement of clinical procedures, it has left the area of communicative competence (as a *comprehensive* view of message–sending) almost untouched.

> The concentration on mastering syntax produced a regrettable tendency in language clinicians to require that children produce complete sentences [all of the time] rather than the elliptical or fragmentary responses that are typical of ordinary dialogue. The aim of clinical intervention is to promote the child's ability to use language effectively. . . . The problem is not that training syntactic constructions is wrong, but rather that it is not enough (Rees 1978, p. 260).

Bates (1976) expressed similar concerns to those of Rees (1978). Structural training should not occur in a vacuum, but rather be part of interpersonal communication skill development. "All of semantics and syntactics are derived ultimately from pragmatics. . ." (Bates 1976, p. 426).

When communicative context is ignored, the clinician is apt to end up with a case like that reported by Geller and Woller (1976, p. 1):

> After having been trained in the therapy room with appropriate stimuli to ask "Who is it?", "What is it?" and "Where is it?", the clinician decided to test Jeffrey's ability to use these questions in a more natural, real–life situation. Jeffrey was told that he and the clinician were going for a walk and he was reminded to ask questions when he got outside. At this point Jeffrey opened the door, stepped outside the building and announced to no one in particular — "Who is it?" "What is it?" "Where is it?"

This example is particularly potent because it is not a "hypothetical horrible"; it really happened! This incident illustrates that unless a child understands the *semantics* and *pragmatics* of syntactic constructions that he is requested to produce in drill, the structure does not become an effective component in his striving for communicative competence. Just as the clinician has the right to know why certain methodologies are being recommended, the child needs to know the *purpose* of learning certain structures. With reference to the case noted above by Geller and Woller, the clinician must first establish the reason for asking learning questions. For example, "We ask questions to get information — to find out about the world. I want to know more about your family, so I'm going to ask you some questions:

> Do you have a sister?
> What is her name?
> How many people are there in your family?
> Who does the dishes at your house?"

After the purpose of questions has been established, then the clinician might say, "When we ask questions, words are in a certain order. Watch." (The clinician has blocks with one word on each. As the word is uttered, the block is sequenced.) The child should then develop an awareness of the semantics of "who," "what" and "where," so that the appropriate word can be retrieved to meet his needs. In other words, the child needs to learn that "who" is used to ask about people, "what" to ask about things, and "where" to ask about places (or locations). The clinician might drill on the word order of each, but at the same time the semantic intent of each "Wh-word" should be emphasized. The clinician might then suggest that the child be "teacher" and test the clinician. A series of stimulus cards (or objects) could be combined that would require that the child assume the linguistic burden of choosing the correct Wh-word. In other words, when looking at the stimulus item, the child would have to decide whether he needed to as the clinician, "*Who* is it;", "*What* is it?" or "*Where* is it?" Extending the contexts for use of these questions, the child might next look at some family and travel photos belonging to the clinician. It has been the author's experience that these will quite readily elicit questions from children in their quest for information about the clinician (or any teacher). Children are naturally curious; it is curiosity that prompts questions. We must, therefore, capitalize on that curiosity.

The clinician in Geller and Woller's example took the child outside to carry over his new interrogation skills. The child was reminded to "ask questions" when he got outside; he took this statement literally. He stepped out the door and recited three interrogative constructions. It is suggested that the clinician's emphasis was not appropriate. The clinician should have stressed the *situation,* not the structure. For example, "We're going out to see what we can learn about our school and the people in it." Perhaps the clinician could begin the questioning. "I don't know where your room is located. Where is it?" If a staff member is observed, the clinician might prompt the child with "See if I know that person." In other words, the clinician should begin syntactic training within a semantic–pragmatic context so that the child has a purpose for learning the structure. As generalization activities are formulated, again try to imagine contexts in which the child would use the particular structure, and then create that context (to the best of your resources) so that the child can practice the newly learned skill.

Part of every therapy session should include a time for dialogue between the clinician and the child (or children). Even when certain lesson segments might be primarily drill-oriented (such as learning to produce a phoneme in various phonetic contexts), some of the therapy session should be reversed for discourse. Children should come to view language as a shared social system with rules for correct use in given contexts. In other words, there are syntactic, semantic and pragmatic rules, and the knowledge of them and the ability to apply them are what Hymes (1971) referred to as "communicative competence." This notion is contrasted to the more restrictive notion of "linguistic competence," which Dale (1976) described (from a transformational grammar model) as the set of learned principles that a person must have in order to be a speaker of the language, which is a focus on the individual's tacit knowledge of the language system.

Carryover

Ideally, the clinician can rely upon parents and teachers to extend stimulus control (or provide supervised generalization experiences). When this is possible, it is recommended that the suggestions be very realistic and that the clinician provide necessary materials. For specific references to aid the clinician in implementing carryover activities with parents and teachers, see Bush and Bonachea (1973) and Simon (1977).

To summarize Premise IV, language teaching cannot be superficial. New learning must be stabilized at an automatic level so that the individual can quickly and naturally retrieve the articulation or language skill learned. In addition, linguistic (phonological, morphological and syntactic) rules must be embedded within a semantic and pragmatic base. Generalization of learned behaviors occurs when the individual acts with purpose and ease in a variety of communication contexts.

PREMISE V

Communication correlates (speaking, listening, reading and writing) should not be artificially separated. Both readiness and reinforcement properties of each should be considered.

Language is the code system for communication; communication manifests itself in speaking, listening, reading, writing and paralinguistic modes. As students, children spend six hours per day for 175 days per year (or approximately 1050 hours each year) engaged in speaking, listening, reading and writing. In particular, large sections of the school day are devoted to the two receptive correlates, listening and reading.

There is evidence that interrelationships among these communication skills exist. Burrows and Neyland (1978) found significant relationships between a child's language comprehension skills and his reading skills. Wiig and Semel (1976, p. 15) note "Combined findings [from various studies] suggest that measures of linguistic abilities relate most closely to measures of reading comprehension and that deficits in language processing may be associated with reductions in reading comprehension."

Premise V will focus on the two receptive correlates (listening and reading) with attention to how general cognitive-linguistic capacities are related to performance adequacy in each.

Language and Listening Skills

Students spend many of their classroom hours listening. They listen to oral directions for written work, for controlling their behavior, and for reading assignments. Comprehension of spoken language (or assigning meaning to phonemic, morphemic and linguistic units) depends upon accurate analysis and synthesis at all levels of processing — the perceptual, linguistic and cognitive-semantic levels. Efficient processing of auditory language requires the ability to process simultaneously at these three levels in addition to the ability to shift between simultaneous and successive processing.

Wiig and Semel (1976) have devoted considerable time and attention to describing the components of receptive language skill. They describe language processing as a complex act composed of:

1. the perception of sensory data.
2. linguistic processing of phonological, morphological and syntactic structure as well as semantic aspects.
3. cognitive-semantic analysis and interpretation, which includes processing
   a. auditory-symbolic cues (phoneme sequences).
   b. semantic units (words and concepts).
   c. semantic classes (verbal associations).
   d. semantic relations (verbal analogies and linguistic concepts).
   e. semantic transformations (redefinition of concepts).
   f. semantic implications (such as cause-effect and prediction).

"Efficient processing of auditory language occurs simultaneously at all [three] levels and it places demands upon auditory attention, short- and long-range memory, feedback and evaluation" (Wiig and Semel 1967, p. 24).

Wiig and Semel's description of the processing task is really an elaboration of Luria's (1973) suggestion that three basic neuropsychological processes are involved in processing and interpreting language with any degree of complexity:

1. retention of elements of sentences;
2. simultaneous analysis and synthesis of the elements; and

3. active analysis of the significant elements to detect the hidden, underlying meaning of the problem stated (as in a mathematical "word problem" or an account of an unpleasant encounter).

Through the speaker's choice of words, meaning is inferred by the listener. Listener ability to interpret the speaker's message is comprised of a composite of skills. Deficits in that composite can have far-reaching effects. "The ability to process, interpret and respond to complex verbal input and information influences the potential for academic achievement, the quality of interpersonal interaction and the potential for social and professional growth. Deficits in verbal comprehension may limit growth in all of these areas" (Wiig and Semel 1976, p. 42).

There are two ways in which the speech–language clinician can provide support for the development of adequate language processing skills:

1. include language processing development objectives in a child's IEPs, or

2. work with classroom teachers to increase awareness of language processing factors and how they can be monitored.

The reader is encouraged to consult Wiig and Semel (1976) for specific suggestions on developmental activities. Their treatment of this subject is so complete that it would be redundant to devote much time to remediation of language processing deficits in this monograph.

The author offers only two general language processing program considerations:

1. Develop the student's awareness of his listener role and his responsibility for providing the speaker with any feedback necessary to obtain a clarification of a faulty message. Students should be given some exercises to practice their processing of language, but they should also learn to evaluate whether the speaker has or has not provided sufficient information. For example, the clinician can place a series of objects on the table, some which are identical. Give a direction such as, "Hand me the house." The student responds, perhaps, by handing the clinician three houses. "No, I said hand me *the* house." The student might say, "But you didn't say which one." The clinician could then respond, "That's right. I gave you a poor direction. What should you have asked me?" The object is to encourage evaluative, heuristic and interactive skills. Teachers are not infallible. Sometimes a teacher does not provide sufficient information for a student to complete the task according to how the teacher has conceptualized it. Before trying to assume what the teacher means, the student should clarify what he understands and what he does not understand. The details needed can then be provided.

2. Consider organizing a discussion group composed of language–involved students who have above–average IQs. Many of the "learning disabled, marginal communicators" fall into this category. Simon (1979) describes the use of a Philosophy for Children program that develops critical thinking, language processing and discussion skills. Such a program requires that the participants listen to the analyses and comments of others and logically manipulate linguistic symbols. For example, a controversial reasoning problem might be used as the basis for discussion:

> Bruce has long hair.
> Hippies have long hair.
> Conclusion: Bruce is a hippie.

The students have to consider accuracy of the statements (*Do* all "hippies" have long hair?) and then critique the validity of the conclusion (Is there enough information available to suggest that Bruce has adopted the lifestyle of a particular culture?). This type of activity helps to develop evaluative skills on the basis of auditory processing of the discussion details and it also forces students to maintain the topic of the discussion. Cognitivie, receptive and expressive skills are developed simultaneously.

In regard to increasing teacher awareness of how linguistic processing components can be monitored and thus controlled to meet age or individual needs, notations by Lasky and Chapandy (1976) will be highlighted. They isolate the following factors that affect language comprehension: syntactic complexity, semantic knowledge, interaction between syntactic complexity and semantic knowledge, contextual cues, and rate of presentation. Frequently these factors are not sufficiently considered during teacher training or when textbooks are written.

Syntactic complexity is defined by Lasky and Chapandy (1976) as the number of transformations necessary to get from deep structure to surface structure. Complexity can be increased, for example, by making an active sentence into a passive sentence (Jane hit the ball/The ball was hit by Jane), adding a negative (The ball wasn't hit by Jane), expanding the noun or verb phrase (The dilapidated ball wasn't hit by the second batter, Jane Jones), or by combining or embedding, or both, two or more ideas into one sentence (When her technique was rusty at the beginning of the season, the dilapidated ball wasn't hit by the second batter, Jane Jones, but by the fourth game, she hit that old ball into the stands).

Semantic complexity refers to the vocabulary used. What a child knows about the words used in a statement will greatly affect his comprehension. For example, the child might not know the word "dilapidated." Unless the redundant adjective "old" were used, message comprehension would be affected in the construction provided in the above paragraph.

Interaction between syntactic and semantic complexity affects comprehension because the child is simultaneously manipulating two difficult types of input. For example, the child might not have been able to even use the redundant adjectives ("dilapidated" and "old") because the complexity of the syntax caused interference.

Lasky and Chapandy (1976) analyzed the complexity of syntactic/semantic interaction in various textbooks written for children in the early grades (and probably used by older, learning-delayed children as well). In a pre-primer, for example, they found that the textbook authors had suggested the following discussion question for teachers to ask, "How do you think Betty and Tom feel about what Father is doing for Susan?" Following their research on complexity of language in teacher's manuals, Lasky and Chapandy concluded:

[The] questions and comments listed for the teacher to present to aid comprehension of the passages in the readers seemed to require comprehension of complex syntactic constructions with semantic concepts that appear formidable for primary-level children (p. 164).

Visual cues seem to aid a listener's comprehension. These visual cues provide additional contextual cues. For example, in a study by Bransford and Johnson (1972), subjects who were shown a picture representing the context of a paragraph (before it was read to them) recalled more than subjects who received no cues, partial cues, or cues *after* the paragraph was read to them. A topic sentence can serve much the same function because it focuses attention before specifics are related.

Rate of presentation can affect the quality of comprehension. Berry and Erickson (1973) present data that document the positive effects of reducing speech rate during the presentation of test items, and Lasky and Chapandy (1976) cite research on the improved comprehension observed in learning disabled students when speech rate is reduced. "Rate of presentation can be altered by slowing the total rate of words per second presented in the message or by inserting pauses between the noun phrase and verb phrase of a sentence, within the verb phrase, or between the verb and the following noun phrase" (Lasky and Chapandy 1976, p. 166).

Language and Reading Skills

Three factors will be considered here:

1. Whether the maturity of a child's oral language comments on his readiness for reading;
2. Whether a child's knowledge of the linguistic system affects comprehension of increasingly complex language (syntax and concepts) used in textbooks; and
3. Whether there is justification for the speech–language clinician spending therapy time helping a child conceptualize the relationships among speaking, writing and reading.

Readiness. There seems to be a compulsion to make all children learn to read by the end of first grade — or even sooner. A child may enter first grade and say to his teacher, "My name is Randy. I six year old." This linguistic output is often ignored and the child is plugged into the reading program advocated by the school system. Once again, research strongly suggests that language development (when needed) should precede the introduction of printed materials (O'Brien 1973). We know that, as a psycholinguistic process, reading is parasitic on language (Kavanagh 1968).

Monroe (1965) discussed the relationship of oral language specificity and organization to the child's readiness for reading as demonstrated through his skill in interpreting pictures. Verbal responses were classified by Monroe on a continuum of one to five, according to the level of interpretive and expressive skill shown:

1. The child merely shrugs his shoulders and does not reply. He may venture to name some of the objects in the picture (e.g., "dog," "boy," "It's a kitten").
2. The child describes what the characters are doing (e.g., "The dog's jumping up." "The baby's eating.").
3. The child expresses a relationship between the characters or objects. ("The boy's playing ball with a dog.")
4. The child sees the picture as one part of a narrative. He gives relationships of time, place, cause and effect. ("The boys are building a birdhouse. They will put it up in a tree so a bird can build a nest in it.")
5. The child reacts to the mood of the picture, perceives the emotional reactions of the characters, and draws a conclusion or evaluates the action. ("This picture's about camping. It's a dark night and the children are kind of scared. They're singing songs around a campfire. Wild animals won't come near a fire.") (pp. 45–46)

Monroe postulates that children who have not reached level three or four on this scale have not developed sufficient language ability to interpret a picture in a primer and to react to the text that accompanies the picture. As Hammer–Eden (1969) points out, Monroe's level three is the first level at which the use of a movable occurs. She hypothesizes (and goes on to demonstrate in her own study) that until a child has reached a stage of language maturity that includes the use of movables, he does not have sufficient language ability to succeed in beginning reading experiences. Like Loban (1961, 1963) and Strickland (1962), Hammer–Eden's research indicates that the use of movables in spoken language reveals a child's linguistic maturity. Due to her research conclusions, and those of others mentioned, Hammer–Eden (1969) recommends that an assessment of children's oral language facility be a part of their reading readiness testing and that various teaching methods be considered, with the teacher choosing the one that would build effectively upon the degree of language maturity demonstrated by the child.

Linguistic Knowledge and Comprehension Skills. The efficient reader must possess two types of linguistic abilities (Mattingly 1972):

1. Primary linguistic activity, comprising the ability to apply a set of internalized, unconscious rules to the processing, comprehension and production of language.

2. Linguistic awareness, comprising the ability to talk about or reflect on language, to segment spoken language into phoneme sequences, and to handle written text in alphabetic form.

"As graphic–phonic cues are processed more effectively, the syntactic and semantic information assumes greater importance in the reading process" (Wiig and Semel 1976, p. 10).

According to Levin and Kaplan (1971), efficient readers process graphic material in terms of phrase units based on structure and not word by word. They "chunk," in other words, in terms of the meaning that is coded in the syntax. Levin and Kaplan concluded that the efficient reader formulates tentative interpretations or hypotheses about the material and confirms or rejects the interpretations on the basis of additional information acquired through grammatical structure and semantic content.

Reddell (1965) studied the effects of similarity between structural patterns in oral and written language on the reading comprehension of fourth graders. Findings indicated that reading comprehension scores on written material that used structural patterns of high frequency in the oral language of fourth graders were significantly higher than reading scores on materials using low frequency patterns. The researcher concluded that reading comprehension is a function of the similarity between language structure patterns in written materials and in the child's spontaneous oral language. Loban (1961, 1963), in a six–year longitudinal study, failed to find a significant relationship between complexity of oral language use and reading abilities in grades one and two, but he did find an increasingly significant relationship in the next four grades. At the sixth grade level, oral language use was an extremely significant predictor of both exceptional reading success and exceptional failure.

It is possible that the research of Lasky and Chapandy (1976) could help to explain Loban's findings (as well as Moore's 1971 notations on the interference of Black dialect on STE comprehension after third grade). By the end of third grade (or the third grade reader), the school system assumes that the child has grasped basic reading skills and begins to concentrate on comprehension of content. The content becomes quite sophisticated as geography, history and science are studied. The syntax is not purposely simplified in these subject area texts. In other words, texts are written primarily by middle- and upper–middle–class professionals from the dominant culture. Their selection of content reflects their status and their expectations (i.e., that school–aged children are not still involved in learning the standard communication code). Strickland (1962) also discusses the relationship of oral language complexity with reading ability and considers intervening variables such as the child's mental age and the educational/occupational status of the parents.

Clay (1969) noted that children with language problems appear to experience difficulty in predicting constructions likely to occur and in noticing the redundant cues that signal that errors have occurred. The regularities of the language code, in other words, are not made use of as cue sources. Vogel (1976) studied the language skills of dyslexic children (in addition to including a comprehensive review of the literature discussing relationships between reading and expressing language skills as well as auditory processing of language). Vogel found that dyslexic children displayed an inability to efficiently use the semantic information available to them because of syntactic deficiencies. In addition, 75 percent of the variance between her experimental (dyslexic) group and the control group (normal readers) could be explained in terms of syntax, semantics and decoding abilities, which she interpreted as confirming the psycholinguistic theory of reading and the importance of syntactic information in reading comprehension.

This strong relationship established by researchers among knowledge of morphology and syntax, oral language, auditory processing, and reading skill certainly indicates that children who are experiencing language deficiencies need development programming prior to or at least concurrent with their reading instruction. They must become aware of how *they* can linguistically map their own perceptions and thoughts prior to undertaking the task of decoding the perceptions and thoughts of others.

O'Brien (1973) discusses "problem–centered reading" as a method of synchronizing observation, listening, speaking and reading through focusing upon environmental concerns as the basis of program content. "It is a highly personal, individualized approach that can serve as a bridge between the child's out–of–school experience and his in-school learning experiences if it is modified to meet particular situations and extended to include other strategies" (p. 105). Halliday (1978) suggests that we have to build up an image of language that enables us to look at how people actually do communicate with each other and how they are constantly exchanging meanings and interacting in meaningful ways.

> If reading and writing are unrelated to what the child wants to mean [or] to the functional demands that he is coming to make of language, they [reading and writing] will make very little sense to him. . . . Reading and writing should not seem like meaningless exercises. They should make sense, matching the child's experience of what language is and what it's used for so that he sees these as a means of enlarging that experience (Halliday 1978, p. 206).

Not only in reading texts can the interaction of syntax, semantics and context affect comprehension. Any specialized subject matter has its own set of concepts. Mathematics, in particular, seems to present some complex challenges because of the emphasis upon the logical manipulation of language. Children having difficulty with communication can be expected to have difficulty with the symbols of mathematics. Chon (1971, p. 326) reminds us:

> As numbers and their generalized algebraic forms are used as a specific language to establish logical relationships for mathematics, the individual with general difficulties in operating with symbols can do math with no more facility than he can handle other elementary language forms.

Aiken (1972) mentions that the specialized language of mathematics differs from social English in that it has a high conceptual density factor reflected by limited, if any, redundancy. "This factor requires that the exact meaning of every concept [word] and logical–syntactic relationship must be discerned accurately since interpretation is not facilitated by the presence of additional semantic–syntactic cues [redundancy]" (Wiig and Semel 1976, p. 15).

Linville (cited in Wiig and Semel 1976) manipulated the variables of syntactic and semantic complexity as they related to ease in solving a math problem. His research design examined:

1. easy syntax and easy vocabulary,
2. easy syntax and difficult vocabulary,
3. difficult syntax and easy vocabulary, and
4. difficult syntax and difficult vocabulary.

The results indicated significant performance differences in favor of easier syntax and vocabulary, with vocabulary level perhaps being more crucial than syntax.

Obviously, textbook authors are not considering these data! Lasky and Chapandy (1976) found that in one first grade math workbook, twenty-six concepts (such as colors, prepositions and specific vocabulary items — sphere, triangle, cylinder and others) were introduced in the first six lessons (or the first seven pages). In another first grade math workbook, they noted these examples of complex semantic concepts embedded in complex syntactic structures:

1. "We are going to pick a card from each set and write a number sentence to tell the number of circles on the cards we have chosen."

2. "How do you think we can find, without counting, if there are as many books in the set of books as there are in the set of chairs?"

3. "If you lived in one of the houses across the street from the playground, where would you cross the street to get to the playground?" (Lasky and Chapandy 1976, pp. 164–65).

In summary, those factors that affect comprehension of language should be taken into consideration. Lasky and Chapandy (1976) offer these suggestions to teachers, clinicians and editors:

1. Use simpler syntactic constructions if the semantic load is more difficult. Gradually build up the syntax, using the semantic items (p. 167).

2. Do not assume comprehension of semantic concepts by automatically inserting these in complex syntactic constructions. Comprehension of semantic concepts should be evaluated in simple as well as complex syntactic constructions (p. 165).

3. Use contextual cues; that is, visual cues and word cues, or verbal redundancy (p. 167).

4. When presenting material orally, slow the rate of presentation by inserting pauses between the major components of a phrase; for example, "John, Jim and Mary (pause) will be going (pause) to the large department store" (p. 167).

Use of Therapy Time to Coordinate Communication Skills. In therapy the clinician should strive to bring the communication correlates more closely together for the child. The child should learn to conceptualize that:

What I can think about, I can say.
What I can say, I can write.
What I can write, I can read.
I can read what I can write and what others have written for me to read.
(Van Allen and Van Allen 1970, p. 21)

One way of doing this is to have the child tell a story about his experiences or a set of sequential pictures. The clinician can ask questions that elicit various movables and clauses. For example:

Child: They're walking.
Clinician: Where?
Child: In that house.
Clinician: Does it look like a regular house or a haunted house?
Child: Haunted house.

As the story is being told (and embellished by the elicited details), the clinician types it for the child.

Clinician: You've told me (begin typing) "They're walking into a haunted house."

The child is then asked to read his story. Even children who cannot read textbooks will be able to read these printed words that they have just dictated. Such experiences reduce the mystery of the written word; after all, it is just speech written down! (See Appendix 16 for an example.)

For some of the older, more advanced language cases (like "marginal communicators"), the author asks the student to tell the sequential story in a particular tense. For example, "This story happened last summer. Tell me what happened last August." After the student tells the story and the clinician has typed it, it is analyzed for past tense cues (auxiliaries, —ed markers and irregular past tense verbs). Wiig and Semel (1976) have presented a convincing argument, buttressed by numerous research findings, that the ability to analyze structural cues aids comprehension of written and spoken information. By engaging in the above-mentioned procedure, the clinician is working on three of the four communication correlates simultaneously. While the student is not writing his own story, he is observing the clinician commit his words to paper.

It is suggested that those of us who are involved in communication take an active role in monitoring the language in textbooks to ensure that instructor disabilities are not misinterpreted as learning disabilities. Unless teachers are aware of the comprehension task complexity, they will not be able to adequately evaluate the materials they are using nor to modify their instructional style to accommodate the needs of their students.

To summarize Premise V, as an individual speaks, listens, reads or writes, multiple components of the communication network are interacting. Analysis and synthesis of cues are constantly occurring. For the child to be a competent communicator, all facets of the communication network should be interacting in a supportive manner. If there is a "weak circuit" in the network, developmental programming is indicated and will, perhaps, serve as readiness for another component of the network. The child's "communication self-concept" can be improved if he feels a growing comfort with the linguistic system and if his teachers adapt materials and instructions to reinforce his growth rather than to continue his frustration with the communication correlates.

CONCLUSION

Five premises have been presented that describe the author's philosophical and procedural bases for her approach to language evaluation, therapy and generalization (or carryover). The intention has been to stress the importance of a functional approach to language when attempting to analyze and develop communicative competence. The clinician must first generate a conceptual model of communicative competence versus communicative incompetence. From this reference point, evaluation and therapy strategies can be instituted. The next section will present examples of incompetent communication.

SECTION IV
Examples of Incompetent Communication

INTRODUCTION

Throughout Sections I through III, "communicative incompetence" has been described. Beginning with Table 1, the author has attempted to synthesize theoretical and empirical information that would help to describe the comprehensive nature of expressive language disability.

The purpose of Section IV is to provide specific examples of incompetent communication. These have been extracted from the professional literature and the author's caseload at the Devereux Day School in Scottsdale, Arizona.

There are three ways in which these examples might be of value to the clinician:

1. To provide examples of behaviors that were heretofore being covered in narrative.

2. To provide some ideas for evaluation techniques.

3. To provide some examples of language sample notations that can be made when the transcription is analyzed.

The first twelve examples of incompetent communication are composites of a variety of cases. The last four examples are more lengthy excerpts from individual case transcriptions.

EXAMPLES OF INCOMPETENT COMMUNICATION BEHAVIORS

Example 1: Restricted Versus Elaborated Codes

Bernstein (1964) defines restricted and elaborated codes as a contrast between context-bound communication (restricted code) and communication that is more free of immediate nonlinguistic context (elaborated code).

Subjects: five-year-old children.

Task: The subjects were given a series of four pictures that told a story and then were asked to tell the story.

Elaborated Code:
1. Three boys are playing football and one boy kicks the ball and it goes through the window   the ball breaks the window   and the boys are looking at it   and a man comes out and shouts at them because they've broken the window   so they run away   and then that lady looks out of her window   and she tells the boys off. (Note: number of nouns — 13; number of pronouns — 6.)

Restricted Code:
2. They're playing football   and he kicks it and it goes through there   it breaks the window and they're looking at it and he comes out   and shouts at them because they've broken it   so they run away   and then she looks out   and she tells them off. (Note: number of nouns — 2; number of pronouns — 14.)

73

3. They're playing ball   it goes through there   he's angry at them and so is she. (Note: number of nouns — 1; number of pronouns — 5.)

Explanation: With the first story the reader does not have to have the four pictures that were used as the basis for the story, whereas in the other two stories the reader would require the initial pictures in order to make sense of the story. The first story is free of the context that generated it, whereas the other stories are much more closely tied to the context.

Example 2: Subordination as an Index of Language Maturity

NOTE: The use of subordination is an index of maturity in language. Effective language needs organization.

Subjects: six–year–olds

Immature Subordination of Ideas: The boy and girl are making a pumpkin and they're playing with the puzzle and uh and its flowers and books.

More Mature Subordination of Ideas: They're playing with puzzles and they're opening up a pumpkin.

They're sitting at the table where there are books and flowers and the pumpkin's there too.

Explanation: Both are describing the same picture and getting much the same thoughts from it, but the more mature child has organized her communication so that it has coherence and so that certain ideas are subordinate to others. The immature child's presentation had no plan and she was not aware of subordination in making her communication orderly, complete and effective. The use of subordination and connectors increases with age, mental age and socioeconomic status (Hammer–Eden 1969, pp. 117–18).

Example 3: Variation in Coherence

The first child, a boy, organizes his communication by subordinating some ideas to others. The second child, also a boy, reveals no plan of presentation; except for a loose chronology, his content lacks the coherence and emphasis necessary to communicate successfully to another person. He is not fully aware of dependent clauses as a way to communicate his ideas.

Subject Y.E.: Well, I was climbing a fence — me and another boy./ He's Chico./ He lives somewhere by us./ A boy pulled on our pants so when we got down we would fall./ So when I went to get down, well, he let go,/ and I jumped down and fell on Chico./ So the boy came around from the fence/ and he started to spit at us/ and we started to run where my daddy was./ But my daddy wasn't there./ He was in the front office,/ and so I told another man that works there./ And the boy went and got a coke and drank it and left./

Subject B.D.: Superman, I seen him last night. . . . Clark Kent is Superman, do you know?/ An he, an he puts a aspirin, you know, a bad man put the aspirin in this little . . . in here,/ an, an he said, and this guy, well he told him . . . an he says how˙ . . . an, an, an this guy pick-pocket him/ and he said, an the man said, "Is that the latest report?/ Let's see."/ An he

74

said, "No."/ This man — see he's a bad man — and the guy he's working for — the boss — well, then he came up and he said, "Give the man some coffee./ Have some for me too."/ And then he went ahead with his money./

Explanation: Although the first subject misses an opportunity to smooth his expression by subordinating his reference to Chico and the location of Chico's home, his discourse is nevertheless coherent. In organizing his material he subordinates four different elements, including one instance of double subordination. Subject B.D., on the other hand, displays little or no plan of presentation for his account of the television program. His language is cluttered with false starts, and only once does he resort to subordination as an aid to organizing his material ("the guy he's working for"). Because he doesn't decide what to feature and what to subordinate, B.D.'s talk lacks plan and order. In terms of features that can be identified and quantified, one major difference between him and Y.E. lies in the use of dependent clauses (from Loban 1961, pp. 96–97).

Example 4: Establishing a Story-Line

One use of language is to compose stories from one's imagination. Observe the difference between the two children's stories below. The first has a story-line, but there are more syntactic/morphological errors. The second is a sputtering of details with no story development, and while there are some structural difficulties, syntax is not the most severe problem. Each child had a box of toys composed of dolls, furniture, vehicles, buildings, etc.

Example I: C.L., age 5.7 (Caucasian male)

Let's make up a story about these guys. Her try to get on that airplane. She tried it. When her sit on there. Off they went. They keep on flying. They so high. They crash and her fall off. They jumped in here. He got up out of here. They had a house. They came out and looked at it. They tried to fix it back up. Someone else fix it up. He couldn't help. He too little. They fix it now. All the people got on the airplane. The plane gonna take off.

Example II: H.D., age 9.0 (Caucasian female)

There was a lady walking in the street. A car was coming over here. Where's the car wash at? This where the car go, right? What's back here? What's it says? There was a lady over the bank. There's a man over the bank. There's a baby was at home. The little girl watch babysitting. There was a horsie parked over home. That's her mamma and that's her dad. There was a lady walking across. The car was drivin'. She runned over. She gotta call the ambulance. She was dead. Cause the car runned over her. When it was yellow and she turned over to — what's this say? — to the jeans store and she picked out a clothes. Who made these things? There's a man walking over here to the street. She's going hospital. He was walking to the sidewalk and there was a car over here. She got a clothes. It's at home. The man walked to a red light, then a car — whoosh — got dead. There was a man coming over to the restaurant to get something to eat. He said what he can do about it and he eat.

Comment: While C.L. had a beginning, middle and end to his story, H.D. was unable to maintain a story plot. She was easily distracted by other stimuli and her own thoughts and instead of composing "a story" she related several isolated incidents and just introduced the characters and described the setting. In addition, there are syntactic and semantic–level construction problems (using incorrect prepositions and combining words in a meaningless way).

Example 5: Interaction of Phonological, Structural and Coherence Problems

Halliday (1973) mentions the informational (or representational) use of language as one of the basic child language functions. There are contexts in which a child is asked (or requests) to tell about an event that has happened (i.e., to represent it for the listener in words). Coherence is an extremely critical feature of this language function. As a speaker relates an event for a listener, there has to be a chronology that maps the interrelationships of the details.

The example below shows the speaker's incompetent use of language to relate an event. There are severe semantic restrictions present, as well as syntactic errors. The speaker is not just incoherent in her chronology of details, but the way in which words are combined to form sentences.

Case: H.D., age 9.0

Clinician Stimulus: Tell me something you did over the weekend.

Child: Brandy was fighting each with Missy and I was watching TV with Tom and Jerry — this afternoon. Tom was hitting Jerry on TV. He took a stick and hit Jerry on the head and then Emergency. Johnny Cage is walking over here to—ah—to Roy and he said, "Can you see we did?" The house fired and somethings. Johnny Cage walking to Roy and he said, "Is that thing — you know those dongs made em wake up — eat the food — and then the dong made em get up on — get out of the chair and get on the fire truck. Ya know that dong thing that make *dong-dong* like that? Makes noise and they . . . Ya know that little bump "sssss" went a back over there — way back over there to get someone that was a sick. When Johnny Cage talked to Roy and he said he almost back there — we almost back over there. And they saw–ed [past tense for see]. We are back there — back over there to someone fixed. No. Johnny Cage and Roy hadda go over there and fix some people. Sick and everything. And the other Johnny Cage hadda go — well ropes and everything to tie the jeep because there was a boy jumped in the hole and made his head get down the hole and his feet was up. That's all.

Comment: This child has a frontal lisp. Obviously, when priorities are established for her programming, articulation should not be considered basic to her communicative incompetence; correction of a frontal lisp should be considered a refinement! Of foremost concern is H.D.'s lack of coherence. Simple tasks such as relating her morning routine before school and telling sequential picture stories can be used to establish an awareness of coherence. Syntactic errors could be corrected through interactive teaching (semantic relationships among words) and drill (obligatory contexts for certain structures).

Example 6: Establishing Semantic Intent

There are some clinical cases who seem to be struggling with the job of linguistically mapping their complex thoughts in a coherent manner. There could be a number of etiological explanations, but that is not the present focus. Two case examples follow that describe this behavior which might be primarily syntactic or semantic.

Example I: J.J., age 6 (5.2 MLU — 68 percent of 73 sentences had restrictions)

Task: "Look at these pictures. They tell a story. You tell me the story."

Restriction Characteristic		
Syn.	*Sem.*	
	X	1. One with all that plates thing.
X		2. What happen?
X		3. Goin' get some stuff right here.
	X	4. He's going a grocery store. (woman pictured)
	X	5. It's going to fall that log right there that bicycle.
	X	6. It's gonna long round thing.
	X	7. That big old bar's that big old thing round thing.
		8. See the log going down the hill.
	X	9. Goin' see that log's going down there.
	X	10. What happen is his bike?
	X	11. That big old log thing — a bike.
X		12. It's a boy going in a house fix his knee.
	X	13. Hurt the bike — the log.
	X	14. Girl — it's going eats some breakfast.
X		15. He get up in the morning and goes a classroom.

Example II: P.F., age 9 (4.21 MLU — 63 percent of 70 sentences had restrictions)

Task: Same as above

Restriction Characteristic		
Syn.	*Sem.*	
	X	1. They are building. (one boy in picture)
	X	2. I washing his face. (girl washing herself)
X		3. One day he putting on the boots.
X		4. Sliding the sled.
	X	5. They bump it 'cause they hurt your knee. (boy's bike hit a log and the boy fell off, hurting his knee)

Task: Tell me why these things go together.

Restriction Characteristic		
Syn.	*Sem.*	
	X	1.' (saddle/horse) Saddle and the horse.
X		2. (cone/ice cream) Cone and the ice cream — put it on the cone.
	X	3. (coat/hanger) Put the coat and put it in the hanger.

Comment: The initial therapy goal with cases like this is for them to learn to encode their thoughts coherently in a series of simple sentences. The therapist needs to decode incoherent statements and provide a coherent model. Once they learn base structure, then they can begin combining thoughts.

Example 7: Verbal Mazes

In judging the fluency with which a person constructs his message, it is possible to evaluate the number of "mazes" found in his message and how characteristic "mazes" are of his communication style. A "maze" refers to a person's confused or tangled use of words when attempting to express a message. Mazes are characterized by many hesitations, false starts and meaningless repetitions. These linguistic troubles resemble very much the physical behavior of a person looking for a way out of an actual spatial maze. He thrashes about in one direction or another until, finally, he either abandons his goal or locates a path leading where he wishes to go. Sometimes he stumbles upon a way out; sometimes he has presence of mind enough to pause and reason a way out. Linguistic mazes consist of a series of words or initial parts of words that do not add up to meaningful units of communication. Sometimes the mazes are very long, consisting of from ten to twenty or more words or word fragments. Sometimes the individual will persevere with the ideas he is trying to formulate, and he will end the maze with a continuation of his thoughts. Other times the individual simply abandons the ideas, perhaps finding the problem too difficult or tiring to express.

The following are examples of mazes from Loban (1961, p. 25). Mazes are in brackets and the count is also circled.

Transcription of Subject's Actual Language	Communication Units	Number of Words in Communication Units
1. (Short maze at the beginning of a communication unit and integrally related to that communication unit.) ["I'm goin] . . . I'm goin' to build a flying saucer / but I can't think how yet."	2	③ - 9 - 7
2. (Short maze in the middle of a communication unit and integrally related to that communication unit.) "When I was fixin' ready to go home, my mother called me up in the house / an' [an' an' have to] I have to get my hair combed."	2	16 - ④ - 7
3. (Long maze not immediately related to a communication unit. The child apparently drops the whole project as being too complicated for his powers.) "I saw a hunter program last Sunday / [an' he, an' snow time he had to have lot uh, wah–h when he, uh, not too many dogs, he . . .] / and that's all I think of that picture."	2	7 - ⑱ - 9

Example 8: Use of Giant Words

Bereiter and Engelmann (1966) coined the term "giant words" to describe a communication style that runs together multiple words within a sentence. For example, "I want you to come here" (consisting of six words), might sound like "I waya kaer" (consistint of three "words"). While "I" functioned as a distinct word, the other two formulations were giant words. Sentences should consist of sequences of meaningful parts. If a speaker runs words together, or speaks in a series of giant words, his speech becomes nearly unintelligible to the listener. The use of giant words, then, can be a factor in communicative incompetence. Sometimes the etiology for this speech style may be neurological; at other times, it is a bad habit. In either case, the individual should become aware of the listener's need for distinct words and the speaker's responsibility to develop a speech rate and production precision that permits words to serve as meaningful segments of a sentence.

Observe the sentence formations in the case below.

Case: P.U., age 10 (Caucasian male)

Words	Giant Words	
5	3	1. The ⌊*girihwatin*⌋ TV. (The girl is watching TV.)
4	3	2. ⌊*Eena*⌋tato chip. (Eating a potato chip.)
6	6	3. The girl spilled da tato chips.
11	6	4. The girl ⌊*ihgoingesum*⌋ to ⌊*cleanem*⌋ up. (The girl is going to get something to clean them up.)
5	1	5. ⌊*Thadateup.*⌋ (The dog ate them up.)

Comment: When the clinician is analyzing a language sample of a child who engages in giant word behaviors, it is important to look at the sample in terms of what the speaker has *actually* produced. It is recommended that two MLUs be computed for this child: (1) what he meant to say (intended words per sentence), and (2) what he actually produced (normal and giant words). The author uses brackets to indicate the occurrence of giant words (see example above). When "unintelligible" sentences are deleted from a sample, the clinician is losing some valuable information about the child's reliance upon giant words and how his language production is being received by the listener. If a child runs words together so that they do not function as independent units, he should not be given credit for them as independent units (words) in an MLU computation. Remember — analyze the child's output in terms of how the listener has to process it; our focus is on *communicative* competence.

Example 9: Dialogue

When two or more people are engaged in conversation, there is a sending, receiving, clarifying, and embellishing of a message. If an individual changes topic, or the speaker and listener have in mind two separate referents, communication does not take place. The following is an example of a dialogue that displays egocentricity and clarifying questions that attempt to establish communication.

Case: J.F., age 14 (7.0 MLU)

Question: What sorts of jobs do you do around your home?
Answer: Picking up the garbage. I'm tired.

Question: I bet it's been a rough day. I'll tell you what — I'll do your chore for you, but you will have to tell me exactly what I have to do. Okay, you tell me what I have to do to take care of your chore.
Answer: You couldn't.

Question: Let's just pretend.
Answer: It's too hard.

Question: Explain to me what I have to do.
Answer: You have ta clean blocks.

Question: I have to clean blocks? What do you mean?
Answer: You have ta chip em with a tool.

Question: What?
Answer: Have to chip the stuff off. Other people used it and they tore their something off when they built it.

Question:	I don't understand. You told me your chore was taking out the garbage. I don't understand what chipping blocks has to do with taking out the garbage.
Answer:	[When the stuff gets] . . . when the garbage can gets full, then I take it out and put it out in the big garbage can, then I bring it back in the house and go play.
Question:	What's this chipping blocks about? Is this something else you do? Do you help your dad?
Answer:	I do it myself. I chip twenty a day.
Question:	You chip twenty blocks a day? What does that mean?
Answer:	There's some stuff on it and you have ta get all that off [so it'll] so the block will be smooth.
Question:	Oh — this is a job you have after school?
Answer:	I get $10.00 a day.

Example 10: Instructions and Explanations

As the regulatory function of language develops, it is used for providing instructions and explanations of how objects work, how you play a game, or how you arrive at a particular destination. In other words, the speaker is assuming the role of a teacher. In doing so, he needs to keep in mind his listener's need for information that is sequentially presented. Following are some examples of incompetent instructions and explanations.

Example I: 14 years old

Question:	Pretend I'm from outer space. I see this telephone (a picture). I don't know what it is or how to use it. Tell me how to use it.
Answer:	You pick it up. It rings. You talk.

Example II: 14 years old

Question:	Explain to me how this needle and thread go together.
Answer:	You put it in that little hole. You put the things up together and tie a knot.

Example III: 14 years old.

Question:	Explain how the lamp and light bulb go together.
Answer:	Put the light bulb in the thing that you screw it in and then you plug the thing in and there's your light.

Example IV: 10 years old

Question:	(Same directions as Example I for the telephone.)
Answer:	It's called a telephone. That thing goes up. You put one on the ear and one on the mouth. You dial it with your number. The cord stretches. It goes by electrical.

Example V: 10 years old

Question:	(After he listened to an explanation, with diagrams and pictures, he was asked to explain how a tricycle works.)
Answer:	Let's see . . . the tricycle works with the front wheel and two pedals. Bar and handlebars. A pipe that bends and goes another pipe and two wheels and just pedal backwards and frontwards and when you stop you just stop with your feet.

Example VI: 10 years old

Question: Here is a play phone. I don't want you to take the phone apart or touch it. Give me directions — just in words — how to use it. Tell me 1, 2, 3, and so on, in the order of what I need to do to use it.

Answer: Pick up the phone. I mean pick up the handle. Put it in the hand you listen to. Put it in — put it close to your ear. Dial the number.

Question: What do you mean — "dial"?

Answer: I don't know.

Question: (As he starts to show me) Tell me in your words.

Answer: You just dial. You . . .

Example 11: Maintaining a Tense Reference

We are able to tell *when* an event happened largely through control of the verb system. There are key words (such as now, tomorrow, yesterday, later on) that help the listener place a message within a time frame, but most of the responsibility falls on copular/auxiliary verbs, changes of the verb (run to ran), and inflections (—ing, —ed, —s). It is difficult for the listener to comprehend the time frame of a story if the speaker keeps switching tense within sentences or within the message. A child who is comfortable with the tense feature of the system will maintain the time marker throughout a story told spontaneously or will be able to tell a story in any tense the clinician requests.

Example I: Tense reference is inconsistent in a spontaneous story.

Child A: She's watchin TV. She's eatin potato chips. She knocks it over. She went to go get the brush and the dust pan. The dog ate all the chips.

Child B: The girl was watching TV. She spilled ghe bowl of cookies. She got up. She will go the kitchen and gets the dust pan and broom. She get the dust pan and broom and she come back. The dog ate all the cookies.

Example II: With a request from the clinician to set a sequential story within a specific time frame ("Pretend this story happened yesterday/is happening right now/will happen tomorrow"), the child might either ignore the request from the beginning of the story, or change tense during the story, or omit future tense auxiliaries.

Child A: (Tell me what she does each day.) She takes a bath in the evening. Puts her pajamas on. Brush her teeth. Hops in bed. Her dad tells a story. (Note: it is possible that this child has not internalized the —es allophonic variety of third person singular inflection — which is needed when a word ends in —s, —z, —ch, —sh — because the —s/—z varieties are evident.)

Child B: (This story is happening right now.) He rode his bike. (Remember, it is happening *now*.) Oh! He is riding his bike. He hit a log. He is falls off. He hurts his knee. He runs home.

Child C: (This story will happen tomorrow morning. It is in the future.) She will get up. Make her bed. Get dressed. Eat breakfast, then she walk to the bus. She ride the bus to school.

Example 12: Question Transformations

Because permutation, deletion and addition of words and inflections are involved in question formations, some language-deficient children take longer than one would expect (judging from MLU) to learn to transform statements into questions. With the use of a puppet, the clinician can say "P. Mooney, my puppet friend, loves to have people ask him questions. Learn more about him. Ask him some questions." After the student has formulated a few spontaneous questions, then whisper "I want you to ask him some questions for me. Ask him why he always carries an umbrella." Continue to provide statements of advancing complexity. It is easy to determine whether or not the child has control enough of the structural code to fluently transform statements given to him into questions.

Example I: B.C., age 10 (6.26 MLU)

1. Which – this ca – what color this car is?
*2. Which horse is eating?
*3. Where is the baby colt?
4. Is the blue car is the front of the green car?
5. Why the the barn was – where's the barn by the house – which barn . . . (gave up trying).
6. Which, which automobile – truck or car – is the farthest?
7. Is the this mother buying the fruits?
8. What time – What time does it gonna be over?
9. Are the twins is walking holding hands – right by their daddy?
10. Where is the farm is?
11. What time is this meeting will be over?

Example II: S.D., age 13 (6.79 MLU)

1. How much it will cost to build roads?
2. How longer will it be?
*3. What is your husband's name?
4. Why doesn't this rain – rain – don't hardly rain here anymore?
*5. Who is the Vice President of this US?
6. Where are ya going on a vacation this year?
7. Where is the capital of the US is?
8. It will snow this summer?
9. Isn't this gonna snow this summer?
10. Is John Smith will be back next year?

*Question form not restricted.

SPECIFIC CASE PROFILES OF INCOMPETENT COMMUNICATORS

Case 1

Subject: S.B., age 9; described by a psychiatrist as "autistic"

Communication Profile: There seems to be a constraint of some kind on his ability to string together relationships that he sees in pictures. He has a tendency to run words together, which impairs intelligibility; the transcription indicates which utterances were intelligible. Both the inability to meaningfully link words consistently and a "cluttering" speech style need to be monitored and receive programming emphasis.

Examples:
1.   boy . . . bicycle
2.   boy cycle
3.i bicycle
4.   boy
5.i ride bike
6.i fall down

7.i bike fall down
8. hurt knee
9.i run to mama
10.i put on a bandage
11. in bath
12. girl toothpaste
13. girl . . . pajamas
14.i girl on beds
15.i daddy read story
16.i girl asleep
17.i wake up
18. out of dress
19. have breakfast
20.i go bus
21.i walk to class
22. girl . . . books
23. a lady cars
24.i lady have groceries
25.i lady cook the supper
26.i a plate the table
27. eat soup
28.i wash the dishes/plate/wash the dishes (counted as 4 morphemes and 2 mazes)
29. putting sock
30. down/the sled (counted as 3 morphemes)

Legend: i = intelligible
. . . = unintelligible series of noises that were intended by the speaker to be words

Case 2

Subject: T.C., age 8

Communication Profile: He is actively engaged in cracking the cultural code. In May 1977, he showed 45 percent restricted sentences in his language sample, and in May 1978, 28 percent showed restrictions. His major problems are omission of some structural forms and inflections, subject–verb disagreement, prepositional confusion, and unfamiliarity with the irregular verb system.

Examples: (not consecutive sentences)
1. Those girls was laughing at her.
2. She felled and then those girls heard her crying.
3. This girl went running in and getting a blanket.
4. The ambulance came.
5. The one doctor went in back of the ambulance.
6. They got at the hospital.
7. Her mom went go get her and bringed her home.
8. These two girls was happy she was all right.
9. She goes in the kitchen and eat.
10. She goes out and wait at her bus stop.
11. He felled and hurt his knee.
12. His mom went got get a band-aid to put on him.
13. His mom put on his band-aid and then she ran back.
14. He went go get his bike and ride it back home.
15. He mighta had ta fix it.

Note: Children like this need to be reminded through drill activities and later in dialogue to "remember the little words." There is a tendency to slur over infinitives, auxiliaries, prepositions and articles as if they really did not matter. The irregular verb system just needs to be memorized.

In evaluation, elicited imitation tasks are quite sensitive to both the "little words" and the irregular verb system. For example, on the stimulus sentence, "She would have liked to go," a typical repetition would be: "She would like a go." Or, "She brought the books."/"She brung the books."

Case 3

Subject: J.B., age 7

Communication Profile: There is confusion between subjective/objective pronoun usage, inconsistent subject–verb agreement, tense reference is not always maintained throughout a sentence or story, and a tendency toward ambiguous pronoun usage. He needs to remediate the few syntactic problems he has and learn to keep his listener in mind. The prognosis for his responding to "awareness therapy" (pointing out his syntactic and pragmatic responsibilities) is good.

Telling sequential picture stories

Example I:
1. The girl was pickin up the potato chip and it fall over.
2. Her said, "I'd better pick this up."
3. By the time her got back they was all gone.
4. He split.
5. A mom saw it.
6. Mom took a vacuum cleaner and cleaned em up.
7. A little boy was playing Star Wars and saw his dad paintin.
8. It was getting in his eyes so he told his dad why don't you wear my helmet.
9. It would get on the helmet.
10. The little boy gave it to his dad.
11. It work—ed (inflection was not integrated in word)

Example II: Explanations

Question: Give me instructions for using this needle and thread.
Response: You take a string and put in that hole. You, uh, uh, stuff with it, uh, uh stitches.

Question: Tell me why this car and license plate go together.
Response: This is a license. This is a car. A license goes *to* a car (confused preposition usage). So people will know what state he is in. And the cops.

Question: Give me directions for using a telephone. Remember, I don't know how to use it. Tell me 1, 2, 3 – just what I need to do.
Response: You take a thing and put it *at* your ear (preposition usage). You see if her's – anybody talking on it. Then you turn the dials and talk to a person.

Note: He becomes more confused when dealing with the regulatory function than the representational function of language.

Case 4

Subject: T.C., age 12

**Communication
Profile:**   Fluency for this boy is greatly affected by the speed of his speech. At 89 words per minute, the following mazes or redundancies appeared:

1. They was three children and they were both climbing trees.
2. One of them fell down [on his back] — on her back.
3. [They] [and and and] One of the children put a cover on her [and and]
4. There was another one who called the hospital [then and then the]
5. The hospital men [put put put] her in the ambulance and the two other childs [they] stayed.
6. The ambulance went [and and and]
7. The doctors looked at one of her legs which was broken and they put a cast on it.
8. She was walking — [he was walking] with her cast and some crutches.

Comment: With the statement, "Good story. Now take it at a slow enough pace that you don't have to start over again so much," the speech rate of 71 words per minute produced no mazes or redundancies. This is a Mexican–American boy from a bilingual home. As is evident, there is some syntactic confusion (15 percent of his sentences in the entire sample showed restrictions), but what detracts from his communicative competence the most is a lack of fluency that appears to be strongly related to his speech speed.

Appendices

APPENDIX 1
Glossary of Terms

cognition	refers to the process of thought, including thinking, knowing, perceiving, remembering, recognizing, abstracting and generalizing
cognitive uses of language	refers to when language is used to explain, to describe, to instruct, to inquire, to hypothesize, to analyze, to compare, to deduce, and to test
communication	refers to the sending and receiving of messages
competence	refers to having certain abilities and skills for a comfortable existence
communicative competence	refers to an individual having adequate knowledge of the syntactic, semantic, and pragmatic rules of the language and the ability to apply them
content (or contentive) words	refers to those linguistic forms within a sentence that carry most of the meaning (nouns, verbs, adjectives, adverbs, and pronouns)
functor words	refers to those words within a sentence whose grammatical function is more obvious than their meaning and which serve primarily to give order to a sentence (articles, prepositions, modal and auxiliary verbs, and conjunctions)
grammar	refers to the theory of language -- an explanation of how the language system rules work
inflection	an affix (prefix or suffix) added to a base word (*pre*school and schools)
interpersonal communication	refers to the use of language for acquiring information from another person or cooperatively getting work accomplished through exchanging ideas
language	refers to a systematic code of symbols structured with rules that serves the function of communicating thoughts, feelings, and perceptions
language components	refers to the linguistic division of the language:
	•phonology the sound system
	•morphology the smallest unit of meaning
	•syntax word order and structural relationships
	•semantics meaning of words and combinations of words
language form	refers to the structural properties of the system as they appear in a message
language function	refers to the meaningful reason that certain words were combined to form a message in varying contexts

movables	refers to those words within a sentence that broaden meaning and can be shifted to various positions within the sentence for variety in expression •movable denoting place (He is *at home.*) •movable denoting time (She goes shopping *on Friday.*) •movable denoting manner (She walked *quickly.*) •movable denoting cause (She went *because she wanted to see her friend.*) •movable composed of a preposition plus an indirect object (He gave the marble *to his friend.*)
pragmatics	refers to the study of rules governing the use of language in context and the roles played by the communication participants
restricted sentences	a sentence that includes a grammatical error
sentence	refers to a collection of morphemes (meaningful units) placed in a particular order to convey meaning
speech	refers to the articulation of language; spoken language
(generative) transformational grammar	refers to an analytical system developed by Chomsky that considers words and word parts and the rules for combining these in various ways to produce all possible grammatical sentences in a language

APPENDIX 2
Eight Semantic-Grammatical Rules*

1. Agent + Action

This rule states that when a child expresses an action being made by a person or thing (agent), the action word follows the agent word. The agent may include someone or something which is perceived to have its own motivating force and to cause an action or process (Chafe 1970). Most agents are animate ("Mommy," "I," "you," "doggie"), but a few are not, such as the first word in the expression "car go." Words for the action function involve perceived movements as expressed in terms such as "push," "take," "write," "stand up," and "go." Brown (1973, p. 193) reports strong evidence for the agent + action rule in the earliest sentences of several languages. Examples of the rule are "Bambi go," "mail come," and "Daddy throw."

2. Action + Object

When a child states that an action is made upon a direct object, the action word precedes the object word. Brown (1973) defines the object in this relation as someone or something either undergoing a change of state or simply receiving the force of an action. The object may be the name of a person or thing or a pronoun, such as "it" or "that." Brown (1973, p. 193) reports occurrences of the rule in French, German, Korean, and Luo languages as well as in English. Examples of the action + object rule include "see sock," "want more," "push car," and "chew it."

3. Agent + Object

When careful account of the context was taken in analyzing early utterances, Bloom (1970) found occasional cases of an agent preceding a direct object without the action word linking the two. While this two-word combination is not observed in adult speech and is reported by Brown as only of marginal occurrence in reports of child speech, the increasing use of a semantic or contextual approach to analyses of grammar may reveal greater occurrence than has been usually reported. Brown (1973, p. 194) suggests that the agent + object construction may constitute a semantic relational unit, as in the case of a child kicking a ball ("boy ball") or turning a key ("boy key") wherein the agent and object seem to be in direct interaction. This position rule is a striking example of the essential role the context may play in identifying the semantic relations (or meaning) of a given grammatical structure. Examples of the agent + object rule are "Eve lunch" (as when Eve is having lunch) and "Mommy sandwich" (as when Mommy is about to have a sandwich) (Brown and Bellugi 1964).

4. X + Locative

When children use a word indicating where something is located or where an action takes place, the rule governing such relations states that such a word is usually placed in the second position. Thus in this rule, the X generally refers to an entity (thing or person) or an action, but could take a range of traditional grammatical roles. The locative is generally expressed with a noun or adverb (for example, "ball room," "baby chair," "throw here," "put there"). The context or the utterance must generally be observed to clearly determine the funcational relation intended. Brown's survey of studies of several languages (1973, pp. 194–195) suggests two major categories for the X + locative rule: action + locative ("walks street" and "throw here") and entity (usually a noun) + locative ("lady home" and "bottle here").

---

*Reproduced with permission from: J. D. MacDonald and J. P. Blott, "Environmental Language Intervention: The Rationale for a Diagnosis and Training Strategy Through Rules, Context and Generalization," *Journal of Speech and Hearing Disorders,* 39, 3, 244-256 (1974).

5. Negation + X

Schlesinger's position rule for negation states that the word implying negation precedes undetermined word class X for the referent that is in some way being negated. Schlesinger offers the following examples: "no wash," "no water," "no down," "no Mama," and "allgone shoe." According to Bloom's (1970) findings, in early language development children apply the single negation rule to communicate three distinct meanings — nonexistence, denial and rejection. While Schlesinger does not make these distinctions formally, his examples of the rule do include the three semantic intentions.

a. *Nonexistence.* In "nonexistence" the referent is not manifest in the context and there is no expectation of its existence. Often the missing referent has been present in the recent past. Forms expressing this meaning include "no more" and "allgone," as in "no more juice" and "allgone magazine."

b. *Rejection.* In "rejection" the referent is present or imminent and is rejected or opposed by the child. For example, Bloom (1970) reports that one of her subjects said "no dirty soap" as she pushed away a sliver of worn soap. Other examples may include "no soup" and "no outside" to express the apparent intentions of rejecting a bowl of soup or an invitation to go outside.

c. *Denial.* In "denial" the child makes an utterance denying that an actual or supposed assertion was the case. For example, if a mother gives her child a gingerbread man and says "Here's a cookie," the child might reply, "No cookie," indicating his denial of the mother's label for the treat.

Thus, it is recommended that while the same position rule negation + X holds for most statements of negation, the semantic functions of the rule should be separated into nonexistence, rejection, and denial for diagnosis and training. Future research may reveal differences among the three negative functions with respect to their development and susceptibility to training.

6. Modifier + Head

The modifier + head rule specifies that when one word of the utterance modifies the other, the word doing the modifying (modifier) precedes the word it modifies (head). Several reports of the distribution of children's early utterances (Brown 1973) reveal three major classes of modifiers that the child and we must learn to distinguish. The three classes of modifiers are attribution ("pretty boat," "big boy"), possession ("Daddy chair," "my car"), and recurrence ("more book" "more read," "nother coke"). Again, as in the case of negation + X, Schlesinger does not formally state the semantic distinctions within the rule but does include these distinctions in his examples of the rule. Knowledge of the context is necessary to reveal which modifier class expresses the meaning of certain utterances. For example, "baby book" may be a statement of possession (whose book?) or one of attribution (what kind of book?).

a. *Attribution.* The rule specifying the position of the modifier before the word modified may be influenced by the fact that, in adult English, this position rule is hard and fast. However, reports from several languages including English note the reverse order in early sentences of children. For example, while many children make descriptive statements such as "pretty boat" and "big car," it is not uncommon in several languages to find descriptions such as "doggie tired" and "carriage broken." Finding both orders in early speech is not surprising, since many languages (including English) exhibit both the prenominal adjective ("yellow block") and the predicate adjective ("The block is yellow"). Thus, the rule specifying that the modifier precedes the word modified may be most useful in directing the child to the desired adult position form when only two words are used for description. In addition, children do not restrict their modifiers to adjectives (as adults usually do) but frequently use nouns and other structures (as in "Mommy doll," meaning the doll that is a Mommy and not the doll that belongs to Mommy).

b. *Possession.* Statements of possession occur with high frequency and productivity (as evidenced by use in novel situations) in the early speech of several languages. This high occurrence may reflect in children primitive notions of property and territoriality (Brown 1973, p. 195). Consequently, the distinction of possession as a separate semantic class within the modifier + head rule may be useful for diagnostic and training purposes. Examples include "my ball" and "Daddy car."

c. *Recurrence.* As in the case of possession, two-word utterances reflecting the semantic relation of recurrence appear to operate with sufficient frequency and independence to merit separate classification under the rule modifier + head. Early statements of recurrence have different meanings in different cases. A word for recurrence may mean the reappearance of a referent observed. The word indicating recurrence is usually "more" or "another," although another was not used before action words, the second word in two-word expressions of recurrence is usually a noun ("more milk") or verb ("more push"). Brown (1973, p. 190) reports that the case for the "universality" of recurrence in the first sentences is fairly strong. Evidence is available for use of the rule in the earliest sentences in German, French and Korean.

7. Introducer + X

When children notice an object or part of their environment, they often express this attention with an introducer word (such as "this," "here," "see") preceding the word for the referent being noticed. The rule introducer + X takes account of two of Brown's (1970) first sentence types. Nomination (for example, "that book") and notice (for example, "hi belt"). Braine (1971) uses the term *ostensive sentence* for an utterance used to identify names, objects, and such. Miller and Ervin (1964) have observed children using this rule in what they call *demonstrative sentences.*

Any word that serves a simple naming function may be the introducer. The most common introducers reported across several languages (Brown 1973) are: "this," "that," "here," "there," "it," "see," and "'s." The word for X may be of any grammatical class that is the object of notice. Thus, X refers usually to a referent that has been pointed at, looked at, or picked up. Consequently, in this rule, X will usually be in the form of a noun, but words for quantities and qualities have also been reported (as in "that blue" and "here more" [Schlesinger 1971]). Brown (1973) describes two prototypical situations in which this rule is manifest. In one situation someone asks the child "what's that?" as he points to something, and the child replies with a name and some introducer such as "it" or "that" (as in "it doggie"). In the second situation, the child initiates the interaction and precedes the name of the object with a word like "this," "that," or "see" (as in "see doggie").

8. X + Dative

When a child expresses that something is done to someone (for example, given, thrown, said), the word indicating to whom the action is directed (dative) follows the word for the action. Examples in the literature are few, but include "give me" and "throw Daddy" (meaning "throw it to Daddy"). This is the only one of Schlesinger's eight rules that is not included in Brown's twelve first sentence types. It is conceivable that the semantic relation expressed by the rule X + dative may be included within the rule X + locative. Research on the distribution of the rules in normally developing children may clarify the existence of the X + dative rule in children's earliest sentences.

Semantic–grammatical (SG) rules that provide content for the Early Language Intervention Strategy and the early types of sentence reported by Brown (1970) as they correspond to the SG rules (from MacDonald and Blott 1974) are presented in Table 3.

TABLE 3

Semantic–Grammatical Rules

Semantic–Grammatical Rules			
Rule	**Examples**	**Sentence**	**Examples**
1. Agent + Action	Daddy throw car go	agent + action	Eve read
2. Action + Object	throw ball see sock want more	action + object	pat book
3. Agent + Object	Daddy ball Mommy soup (as when Daddy is throwing ball or Mommy is eating soup)	agent + object	Mommy sock
4. X + Locative a. Entity + Locative	ball chair ball there	locative (noun + noun)	sweater chair
b. Action + Locative	throw me throw here	locative (verb + noun)	walk street
5. Negation + X a. Nonexistence	no ball no more ball (as when child finds no ball when he expects one)	nonexistence	allgone rattle
b. Rejection	no ball (as when child is given but doesn't want the ball)	–	–
c. Denial	no ball (as when child denies the assertion that an apple is a ball)	–	–
6. Modifier + Head a. Attribution	pretty boat big boy	attribution (adj. + noun)	big train
b. Possession	Daddy chair my car	possession (noun + noun)	Mommy lunch
c. Recurrence	more book more read	recurrence (more + noun)	more milk
7. Introducer + X	see boy hi dolly it doggie	notice nomination	hi belt that book
8. X + Dative	throw me	no correspondence (may be included in Brown's locative V + N sentence type)	–

APPENDIX 3
Lee's Developmental Sentence Scoring Complexity Index*

Score	Indefinite Pronouns or Noun Modifiers	Personal Pronouns	Main Verbs	Secondary Verbs	Negatives	Conjunctions	Interrogative Reversals	Wh-Questions
1	it, this, that	1st and 2nd person: I, me, my, mine, you, your(s)	A. Uninflected verb: I *see* you. B. copula is, or 's: *It's* red. C. is + verb + ing: *He is coming.*		it, this, that + copula or auxiliary is, 's, + not: It's *not* mine. This is *not* a dog. That is *not* moving.		Reversal of copula: *Isn't it* red? *Were they* there?	
2		3rd person: he, him, his, she, her, hers	A. –s and –ed: *plays, played* B. irregular past: *ate, saw* C. Copula: *am, are, was, were* D. Auxiliary *am, are, was, were*	Five early-developing infinitives: I *wanna see* (want to see) I'm *gonna see* (going to see) I *gotta see* (got to see) Lemme [to] see (let me [to] see) Let's [to] play (let's [us to] play)				A. who, what, what + noun: *Who* am I? *What book* are you reading? B. where, how many, how much, what ...do, what...for, *Where* did it go? *How much* do you want? *What* is he *doing? What* is a hammer *for?*
3	A. no, some, more, all, lot(s), one(s), two (etc.), other(s), another B. something, somebody, someone	A. Plurals: we, us, our(s), they, them, their B. these, those		Noncomplementing infinitives: I stopped *to play.* I'm afraid *to look.* It's hard *to do* that.		and		
4	nothing, nobody, none, no one		A. can, will, may + verb: *may go* B. Obligatory do + verb: *don't go* C. Emphatic do + verb: I *do see.*	Participle, present or past: I see a boy *running.* I found the toy *broken.*	can't, don't		Reversal of auxiliary be: *Is he* coming? *Isn't he* coming? *Was he* going? *Wasn't he* going?	

*Reproduced with permission of the author and the publisher. L. L. Lee, *Developmental Sentence Analysis*, Evanston, Illinois: Northwestern University Press (1974). *(Continued on page 96)*

(Continued from page 95)

Score	Indefinite Pronouns or Noun Modifiers	Personal Pronouns	Main Verbs	Secondary Verbs	Negatives	Conjunctions	Interrogative Reversals	Wh–Questions
5		Reflexives: myself, yourself, himself, herself, itself, themselves		A. Early infinitival complements with differing subjects in kernels: I want you *to come.* Let him [*to*] *see.* B. Later infinitival complements: I had *to go.* I told him *to go.* I tried *to go.* He ought *to go.* C. Obligatory deletions: Make it [*to*] *go.* I'd better [*to*] *go.* D. Infinitive with wh-word: I know what *to get.* I know how *to do it.*	isn't, won't	A. but B. so, and so, so that C. or, if		when, how, how + adjective *When* shall I come? *How big* is it? *How* do you do it?
6		A. Wh-pronouns: who, which, whose, whom, what, that, how many, how much: I know *who* came. That's *what* I said. B. Wh-word + infinitive: I know *what* to do. I know *who(m)* to take.	A. could, would, should, might + verb: *might come, could be* B. Obligatory does, did + verb C. Emphatic does, did + verb			because	A. Obligatory do, does, did: *Do they run? Does it bite? Didn't it hurt?* B. Reversal of modal: *Can you play? Won't it hurt? Shall I sit down?* C. Tag question: It's fun, *isn't it?* It isn't fun, *is it?*	
7	A. any, anything, anybody, anyone B. every, every-thing, every-body, everyone C. both, few, many, each, several, most, least, much, next, first, last, second (etc.)	(his) own, one, oneself, which-ever, whoever, whatever: Take *whatever* you like.	A. Passive with *get,* any tense Passive with *be,* any tense B. must, shall + verb: *must come* C. have + verb + en: *I've eaten.* D. have got: *I've got it.*	Passive infinitival complement: With *get:* I have *to get dressed.* I don't want *to get hurt.* With *be:* I want *to be pulled.* It's going *to be locked.*	All other negatives: A. Uncontracted negatives: I can *not* go. He has *not* gone. B. Pronoun–auxiliary or pronoun–copula contraction: I'm *not* coming. He's *not* here. C. Auxiliary–negative or copula–negative contraction: He *wasn't* going. He *hasn't* been seen. It *couldn't* be mine. They *aren't* big.			why, what if, how come, how about + gerund *Why* are you crying? *What if* I won't do it? *How come* he is crying? *How about* coming with me?

8

A. have been +
verb + ing
had been +
verb + ing
B. modal + have +
verb + en: *may
have eaten*
C. modal + be +
verb + ing:
could be playing
D. Other auxiliary
combinations:
*should have been
sleeping*

Gerund:
Swinging is fun.
I like *fishing*.
He started *laughing*.

A. where, when,
how, while,
whether (or not),
till, until, unless,
since, before,
after, for, as, as
+ adjective + as,
as if, like, that,
than:
I know *where*
you are.
Don't come *till*
I call.
B. Obligatory dele-
tions:
I run faster *than*
you [run].
I'm *as big as* a man
[is big].
It looks *like* a dog
[looks].
C. Elliptical dele-
tions (score 0):
That's *why* [I
took it].
I know *how* [I
can do it].
D. Wh-words +
infinitive:
I know *how* to
do it.
I know *where*
to go.

A. Reversal of
auxiliary have:
Has he seen you?
B. Reversal with
two or three
auxiliaries:
Has he been
eating?
Couldn't he have
waited?
*Could he have
been* crying?
*Wouldn't he have
been* going?

whose, which, which +
noun:
Whose car is that?
Which book do you
want?

*Reproduced with permission of the author and the publisher. L. L. Lee, *Developmental Sentence Analysis*, Evanston, Illinois: Northwestern University Press (1974).

APPENDIX 4
Suggestions for Evaluating Expressive Language Behavior

A. Begin with a gross measure of language performance by collecting a taped sample of language being used for varying purposes.

   1. Introductory dialogue – this is used for identification purposes on the tape (name, age, grade) and not counted as part of the actual sample.

   2. Sequential picture stories (*Before We Read,* by Scott, Foresman and Company) are particularly good because the student has to draw together numerous relationships pictured among people, objects and events.

      a. Spontaneous performance: Say "These pictures tell a story. I want you to tell the story to me."

      b. Cued performance: Say "I have a story about these pictures, too. Listen to my story. When I'm finished, I want you to tell me *my* story. It's a copy-cat game." This component of the evaluation process taps the gap between the child's performance and his competence. (See Appendix 6.)

   3. Dialogue between the clinician and student:

      a. Ask about the student's interests.

      b. Use a variety of wh–questions (who, what, where, why, when, which, how) to assess the student's ability to process the semantics of each question word.

      c. Discuss topics of interest in the school or social issues of concern to the student and assess the student's ability to "maintain the flow of meaning," or sustain the topic.

   4. Construct opportunities to assess the seven functions of child language (Halliday 1973; see page 34 of this monograph for a discussion of Halliday's language functions).

      a. Instrumental

         (1) Have the student face an open cupboard displaying a number of enticing playthings and ask him to describe which he wants to play with when the evaluation is over. Remind him that since the clinician's back is to the cupboard, his description will need to be complete.

         (2) Role–play a student coming up to the manager of a supermarket to ask for an item that cannot be located on the shelves.

      b. Regulatory

         (1) Either through role–playing (with older students) or puppets, set up a situation where the student is in charge of a team project or the house when parents are away, and he has to get you to conform to his requests.

         (2) Ask the student to provide directions for the placement of objects in an activity similar to the Glucksberg and Krauss (1967) research task. Set up a barrier (such as a box) on the table and provide the student and yourself with identical objects (such as various block forms and dollhouse furniture). Give the student three objects and yourself an identical set of objects (for example, each of you might have an orange block that looks like a bridge, a yellow cylinder block and a dollhouse chair). Ask the student to arrange them in some way and to give you directions so that your three objects will be in the same arrangement as his when the barrier is removed.

(3) Have the student give you instructions for using the telephone. Show the student a picture of a telephone and say "We are going to pretend that I have never seen one of these things before. Let's say I'm Mork from Ork and I want to know what this is and how to use it. You will need to give me instructions, 1 - 2 - 3, on how to use this object."

c. Interactional
   (1) The dialogue you had earlier with the student will comment on this language function.
   (2) Using DLM 339 Written Language Cards, role–play the situations pictured.
   (3) Purposely express an unpopular opinion or mention that someone of the student's age expressed the opinion; if the latter option is chosen, role–play the situation and observe how effectively the student communicates when he is agitated.

d. Personal
   (1) Using DLM430 Consequences Cards, ask the student to express his opinion about the various acts (such as throwing garbage in a stream, or hitchhiking) that are displayed.
   (2) Ask a student to tell you what it is about the school (home, members of the family, community) that annoys him.
   (3) Ask the student what his interests are and explore *why* the student enjoys those various hobbies or activities.
   (4) Engage in clarification of values, asking the student to defend his values on such topics as religion, politics, smoking, drugs, participation in war, career–oriented women.

e. Heuristic
   (1) Show pictures of members of your family or photos of trips · these will usually generate many questions.
   (2) Show the child a variety of transportation vehicles, put the eight or ten photo cards down, select one from within the pack and ask the child to question you about the identity of the vehicle chosen. The one question that cannot be asked in this "game" is "What is it?"
   (3) Take a picture from a *National Geographic* magazine, or some other anthropological source, and ask the child to look at the pictures. If questions are not naturally generated, then say "See how much you can find out about these people. I've read about them and I will answer your questions."
   (4) Phone a store for information about a product.
   (5) Probe the degree of complexity with which a student can structure a question. Take out a puppet and say "My friend loves to answer questions. I will tell you what to ask him. Ask him why he always takes his snorkel with him on rainy days." This becomes a highly complex transformation, "Why do you always take your snorkel with you on rainy days?" You can use Lee's (1974) Developmental Sentence Scoring Complexity Index (Appendix 3) as a guide to structuring stimuli for increasing complex questions. This task can only be successful, of course, if the child understands the difference between "ask" and "tell."

f. Imaginative
   (1) Give the younger student a selection of toy people, furniture, cars, a house and a couple of animals (approximately a dozen items). Say "Make up a story for me about these people. You can use all these toys in your story."
   (2) Give the older students a Norman Rockwell picture or one of the Teaching Resources (85–330) Tell–A–Tale cards and ask him to construct a story.

(3) Give younger and intermediate students a flannel board with some traditional fairy tale cut–outs and ask them to tell you the story.

g. Informational (representational)
(1) The sequential picture stories tap this function.
(2) Show the student a sequential picture story, remove the pictures and ask the student to tell you the story.
(3) From your dialogue with the student, you can construct notations on the student's ability to describe his participation in an event he enjoyed.
(4) Ask the student to relate his morning routine or describe an after–school or summer job.
(5) Ask the student to tell simple sequential picture stories (such as those in the DLM127 series) in a variety of tenses, so you can evaluate the student's flexibility in providing time references and his ability to maintain a tense reference throughout a story. Say:
  (a) "This little girl goes through the same routine every morning as she gets ready for school. I want you to tell me what she does each morning." (present tense)
  (b) "This boy went for a bike ride last Saturday. Tell me what happened last Saturday." (past tense)
  (c) "This little girl does the same things each night when she gets ready for bed. She will do these things tonight. Tell me what she will do tonight." (future tense)
  (d) "Look into this Viewmaster (or filmstrip viewer). I can't see what is going on each frame of the story. I want you to tell what is happening in each frame." (present progressive tense)
(6) Have the student explain how two objects go together, such as those in the DLM P159 Motor Expressive Cards (flower/vase; baby/bib; car/license plate).
(7) Read a brief explanation of how a tricycle or bicycle works and have the child explain the process to you. (Make diagrams or pictures of these vehicles available to the child.)
(8) Explain the meaning of proverbs pictured on CSB Communicative Competence cards (1980).

As you begin to work with the student and observe his interactions with peers, additional notations should be made about the student's flexibility in using language effectively to serve a variety of purposes.

B. Consider clinical observations during the evaluation session.

1. Does the child speak at an exceptionally slow rate? This rate might be a sensitive indicator of the child's auditory processing rate as well. It has been the author's clincial experience that a student who speaks at 65 to 80 words per minute (when the adult average is approximately 140 words per minute), is more competent processing oral directions or story content that has been reduced in rate to approximately 100 words per minute. To determine the student's rate of speech, take three separate one–minute segments from his language sample and derive a mean number of words per minute. The author does this after the sample has been transcribed by turning on the tape recording, listening for a minute, and noting the number of words spoken in the transcription during that time. If a student has a particularly slow speech rate, this information is shared with his classroom teacher and it is recommended that when instruction and discourse are directed toward this student, a slower rate of speech be used.

2. Does the student respond accurately to the semantic intent of various wh-questions? Who, what, where, when, why, which, how questions are requesting specific types of information.

3. What is the degree of latency between stimulus presentation and response? For example, on the *Peabody Picture Vocabulary Test,* does the child seem to absorb all four pictures at once or is each looked at for a period of time and then all four studied before a response is given? Research (Morehead and Johnson 1972) has indicated that some children take a longer time than others to produce meaningful images from stimuli presented, for cognitive interpretation. Speed of performance in our culture is valued and frequently this child can be passed over in the classroom because he has not been able to provide an answer as *quickly* as another child. Again, the classroom teacher should be informed that this is a student for whom she/he may need to wait for a minute before response to a question will be forthcoming.

4. Has the student been able to observe cause–effect relationships in sequential picture stories? For example, in the *Before We Read* book (Scott, Foresman and Company), there is a pictorial sequence showing Sally eating potato chips while watching a television program. As she reaches for a chip, the bowl of chips falls on the floor near her dog, Spot. She goes to the kitchen to get a dustpan and brush to clean up the mess. While she is gone, Spot begins eating the potato chips and by the time she returns, the chips are gone. Some children will interpret these character–object–event relationships accurately. Others, however, will look at the final picture in the series (showing Sally with dustpan and brush looking down at the floor where the chips had fallen and noticing that they were gone, but Spot is looking very content) and say "And Sally came back and cleaned up the mess." Obviously, the child has not perceived the cause–effect relationships involved.

5. Does the child tell a flowering story when looking at a sequential picture series, or does he just label the items or the actions in each picture? Monroe (1965) has presented a hierarchy of sequential picture story responses (quoted on page 65 in this monograph) which comments on the child's readiness for reading. This information should also be shared with the classroom teacher.

C. Correlate tests* may be used to supplement the information gathered in the language sample. The evaluation process should always be individualized, with the clinician administering only those correlate tests that provide additional descriptive data upon which programming could be based. In other words, all correlate testing should have an underlying purpose. A battery of tests administered to every child lacks rational purpose and wastes programming time.

1. Phonology — If a student has only a few articulation errors, these can be recorded from the language sample. Make notations on the transcription and transfer this information to the Clinician Worksheet (Appendix 8) under the phonology section.

   a. Investigate error patterns, either through distinctive feature analysis or the more traditional place/manner analysis.

   b. Find "can–do" contexts in which the child can produce the sound; most articulation errors are phonemic rather than phonetic, so it is worth probing for a context in which the child can produce the phoneme and then generalize it to other contexts rather than teach sound production as if the child had formally been unable to articulate it. Many times "can–do" contexts appear in the transcription, but if they do not, consider use of McDonald's *Deep Test of Articulation.*

2. Morphology — By doing a morpheme and a word count for each sentence in the language sample, it can be ascertained whether or not the child is relying upon morphological markers. For example, "the boys play" represents three

---

words, but four morphemes. The plural marker on boys is a meaningful unit marking number. A comparison of mean morphemes versus mean words per sentence is especially revealing for MLUs of under 5.0. By including a section in your sampling procedure where you investigate the student's ability to relate a story in a variety of tenses, you automatically tap time markers.

   a. The Grammatic Closure (ITPA) Subtest produces good information on a variety of morphological markers.

   b. The CELI *(Carrow Elicited Language Inventory)* serves the purpose of showing some markers that might be in transition; while the marker might not be present in the child's spontaneous language or even on a task such as the Grammatic Closure Subtest, the CELI might show that the marker does have sufficient meaning to the child that he can repeat it, when it is modeled.

   c. The TACL *(Test for Auditory Comprehension of Language)* will comment on the child's comprehension of morphological markers.

3. Syntax — While the language sample will indicate which structures the child relies upon, it might not comment upon all the structural combinations within the child's awareness or competence.

   a. The CELI *(Carrow Elicited Language Inventory)* provides an opportunity to assess "emerging structures" and to analyze the error strategies being used by the child (such as omission, substitution). For younger children, interest in the task is increased by making it a game. Give them pieces of Lego (or some other toy consisting of construction units) each time they repeat a sentence. The author always says "We're going to play a building game. Every time you say exactly what I say, I will give you one more Lego." Make sure that the child is looking at you as you provide the stimulus sentence; you can do this by holding the Lego unit close to your mouth while you say "Listen (getting the child's attention), say . . ."

   b. The ELI *(Environmental Language Inventory)* should be used for elicited imitation purposes if the child has an MLU of under 4.0. The author has found the CELI to be a waste of time for the vast majority of cases who are speaking primarily in content words. The ELI will thoroughly tap the semantic–grammatical rules the emerging communicator is using.

   c. The TACL *(Test for Auditory Comprehension of Language)* provides good receptive data on syntax, morphology and semantics because it gives some indication of the child's process S-V-O relationships as well as various concepts (colors, prepositions, Boehm vocabulary). The author uses this test as a screening tool for the BTBC *(Boehm Test of Basic Concepts)* and the ACLC *(Assessment of Children's Language Comprehension)*. If the child does poorly on the TACL "vocabulary" units or processing critical syntactic–semantic elements within a sentence, the BTBC is then administered as well as the ACLC.

   d. The Grammatic Closure (ITPA) Subtest provides good data on the irregular aspects of the language irregular comparatives/superlatives, plural nouns and verbs, and reflexive pronouns. For intermediate level and older students who do poorly on the irregular past tense verbs, a quick conjugation exercise on the fifty most common irregular verbs is provided in which flashcards with the base verb (such as *run*) are shown and then a record is made of those verbs the student can conjugate into the past tense and those he cannot. The author says, "I have some goofy action words here. For example, I *run* today. Yesterday I did the same thing. Yesterday I_____ . Good. *Ran.* Tell me the rest of these." Provide the same stimulus sentences for each verb.

4. Semantics — The appropriateness with which the student combines words into sentences and sentences into descriptions and explanations is tapped in the

language sample. Additional testing that provides baseline data for programming seems to center on vocabulary strength and the logical manipulation of verbal symbols.

    a. Vocabulary development should be considered in terms of breadth and depth (Siegel and Broen 1976).

        (1) *The Peabody Picture Vocabulary Test* provides an indication of the student's receptive vocabulary, but one must be cognizant of its limitations (Nicolosi and Kresheck 1972; Kresheck and Nicolosi 1973).

        (2) *Boehm Test of Basic Concepts* assesses the student's understanding of vocabulary frequently used in teacher and textbook instructions.

        (3) Informally probe the student's ability to organize his lexicon in terms of superordinate classes (transportation) and their subordinates (cars, trains, buses).

        (4) Using *My Life Pictionary — Multiple Meaning Words* (Instructional Industries, Inc.), observe the variation in meaning a word has for a student. For example, the word *draw* — "Draw your gun, cowboy," "They like to draw animals," "The horse is drawing the carriage" — ask the student what *draw* means in these various contexts.

        (5) Assemble a group of pictures of common objects in the student's environment (or use the Peabody Language Development Kit cards or the PRK 101 Photo Resource Kit from Modern Education Corporation) and gather baseline data on how many of these labels the student knows.

        (6) Using *In Other Words* (Scott, Foresman and Company), a student thesaurus, take several base vocabulary words (such as *walk*) and select approximately five synonyms (amble, stalk, shuffle, hike, stroll). Ask the student to first define the synonym and then place the word in a sentence to see if the student can discern the meaning when the word is placed in context. The author has found that teaching vocabulary to learning/language–impaired students is most effective when working within a superordinate–subordinate framework or a base vocabulary reference. By engaging in this initial data gathering on vocabulary scope and depth, it is possible to write productive IEPs and later assess vocabulary growth.

    b. The student's cognitive–linguistic manipulation of the language should be studied.

        (1) Ask students to explain the meaning of captions on various posters you may have in the room (such as the poster showing a cartoon character who looks like a lemonade machine and has lemons going into his head and lemonade coming out of his nose with the caption "If life gives you lemons, make lemonade").

        (2) Have the student explain the meaning of various proverbs and maxims (see *Language Remediation and Expansion — 100 Skill Building Reference Lists* by Communication Skill Builders, Inc.).

        (3) Have the student read a parable (or read it to him) and have him explain the moral.

        (4) Use the Inferences Subtest from the *California Test of Mental Maturity* to assess how well the student can cope with class and conditional logic.

        (5) The Auditory Association (ITPA) Subtest comments on the student's ability to relate concepts verbally.

5. Auditory Considerations — Although it is not the purpose of this outline on expressive language evaluation to describe receptive language considerations in detail, a few general points will be mentioned.

    a. Acuity: as Kleffner (1973) has discussed, a hearing evaluation is crucial for any child referred for a "language problem."

b. Processing: if a child is having difficulty integrating, organizing and remembering incoming stimuli, his world will be confusing and frustrating. Auditory processing considerations should include:

    (1) Wiig and Semel's (1976) suggestions for evaluating the student's competence in dealing with logico-grammatical input, including their *Test of Linguistic Concepts.*

    (2) The student's ability to cope with multiple critical elements in a message, which can be assessed through:

        (a) the *Token Test* (de Renzi and Vignolo 1962), which appears in a variety of informal forms and several new standardized forms.

        (b) The ACLC *(Assessment of Children's Language Comprehension).*

        (c) informal level of command tasks (such as "Stand up, clap your hands, pick up the pencil, and sit down" — a four-level command — or "Draw a one-inch square in the middle of your paper and place a small X two inches above it" — a two-level command with seven critical elements to be processed).

    (3) Lasky and Chapandy's (1976) discussion of the effects of speech rate and syntactic/semantic complexity on comprehension.

    (4) An evaluation of the student's ability to comprehend details and interrelationships mentioned within a story (Rees and Shulman 1978).

6. Evaluation of Classroom Performance Skills — frequently teachers are most responsive to a general "score" that comments upon the student's "language skills." The *Utah Test of Language Development* taps a wide variety of classroom-related skills in a relatively short period of time and has, in the author's experience, yielded a score that is quite representative of the age-level work a student is capable of doing in the classroom. In IEP staffings, this general score is a good reference with which to begin presenting the more detailed findings that are provided through the evaluation procedures described above.

D. Organize accumulated data so that you have a clear picture of what the child can and cannot do during communication.

1. The Hannah Linguistic Development Summary Sheet (Hannah 1977) allows the clinician to make a record of the types of basal sentences and transformations the student relied upon during the language sample. It is possible to add notations about transformations that appeared during correlate testing and note the types of sentence complexity the student has relied upon during the sample. See Appendix 7 for an example of this form.

2. The Simon Clinician Worksheet organizes error patterns that typify the student's ineffective (or deviant) communication. See Appendix 8 for an example. The worksheet is divided into seven sections for specific types of notations:

    a. Reason for Referral: quote the person who referred the student.

    b. General Observations: behaviors such as rate of speech, interest in communication, latency behaviors between stimulus presentation and response, and other behavioral characteristics or response styles that might indicate this student manifests unusual or individualistic behaviors that need special attention in the classroom.

    c. Phonology: comment on specific articulation errors noted in the sample (if more exist than space is allotted for, that probably indicates an articulation test would be advisable); note error patterns and whether or not the student relies upon "giant words" (see Section IV, Example 8).

    d. Morphology: use this section to note word endings that are missing or not being comprehended.

e. Syntax: after you have transcribed the sample, you will have a good idea of the major types of errors the student is showing; note these on the worksheet. In addition, make notes of error patterns on receptive and elicited imitation tasks.

f. Semantics: comment upon the student's vocabulary skills, the appropriateness of his answers to wh–questions, his understanding of concepts presented during testing (such as on the TACL, BTBC), his ability to interpret cause-effect relationships in the sequential picture stories, associative and logical thinking skills and the degree to which syntax in statements and questions maps semantic intent.

g. Interpersonal Communication: make notes on general factors affecting the quality of sending and receiving messages and specific notes on each of the language functions that have been tapped. It may be necessary to add a second sheet which just focuses on the latter.

(1) General factors.

(a) Is speech loud enough to be heard?

(b) Are verbal mazes (see Section IV, Example 7) abundant and how severely do they detract from the semantic intent of the message?

(c) Can the individual rephrase a statement to provide greater clarity or coherence after the listener has requested a clarification?

(d) Is the student's rate of speech easy for the listener to process?

(e) Is the student coherent when explaining details of an event?

(f) Are messages egocentric or sociocentric? In other words, is sufficient information provided so that the listener can comprehend the content of the message, or is the message assuming information the listener does not have?

(g) Are there ambiguous pronoun references (such as "She gave her the package and then *she* left")?

(2) Language functions: notes on each of the seven child language functions that Halliday has described in this monograph (page 34).

3. Add test scores and other gross indicators of performance (such as TACL: 6.8 MA) in the right–hand column on the Simon Clinician Worksheet (Appendix 8). Place the test data under the most appropriate category (such as CELI under Syntax). Circle any scores that are at or above age level. If space allows, specific notations can be made under the most appropriate category regarding specific performance behaviors. If not, make analytical comments directly on the test form (such as the type of items missed on the PPVT or Grammatic Closure Subtest or how the responses on the CELI compared with spontaneous usage during the language sample).

E. Error analysis focuses upon the dominant patterns in the student's communication that make him appear incompetent. By gathering baseline data on these patterns, IEPs can be constructed and future performance can be compared to observe advances made. When analyzing the accumulated data, make gross and fine notations. Place these notations under the most appropriate category on the Simon Clinician Worksheet (Appendix 8). For example:

1. Gross notations provide an overview.

a. Mean length of utterance describes length but not necessarily complexity of language (Lee 1974).

b. Percentage of restricted versus nonrestricted utterances provides an estimate of the degree of syntactic–semantic incompetence.

2. Specific notations are made in terms of the rate of error per obligatory context (such as –*ing* that should have appeared fifteen times, but because of the student's disabled rule system, appeared only eleven times thus producing a 27

percent error rate). Use a calculator to divide the number of errors by the number of obligatory contexts. In the example provided, 4(00) was divided by 15 and produced 26.6, which is rounded to 27 percent. Each student's error patterns will differ, but some of the more common patterns in the author's experience are:

   a. Morphology
      (1) The omission of −ed, −ing, −s (plural, possessive, third person singular).
      (2) The substitution of −ed on base verbs for irregular past tense forms (runned).

   b. Syntax
      (1) The omission of copular and/or auxiliary is/was, articles, subjects, infinitives.
      (2) Substitutions of objectives for subjective pronouns (her/she), singular for plural subject–verb agreement, base verbs for irregular past tense verbs (run/ran), and confusion in usage of *at, to, for.*

   c. Semantics
      (1) Find the percentage of sentences that were restricted for semantic rather than syntactic errors (see Section IV, Example 6).

   d. Interpersonal communication
      (1) Find the percentage of sentences that have verbal mazes in three or more words.
      (2) Find the percentage of adequate versus inadequate explanations for the relationship of two objects (for example, out of five trials, only two were coherent and nonegocentric).

F. It is very enlightening to look at current data in relation to past data on a student. The Longitudinal Evaluation Summary provides an opportunity to make comparisons of data (see Appendix 10).

G. Developmentally sequence those behaviors that need clinical management (see Appendix 12). The author has found it convenient to file an IEP Masterlist (Appendix 12) on each child in her caseload. As an error behavior or incompetent strategy is remediated, it is checked off and programming for the next behavior on the developmentally sequenced list is planned. After some experience, it might be possible to skip this step and just developmentally sequence error behaviors on the Simon Clinician Worksheet. For example, you could make a copy (carbon or electrostatic) of the student's individual case folder (with his evaluation data, progress notes, etc.), and the other copy would be placed in a "master file." The master file would consist of copies of worksheets from each student in your caseload. When constructing lesson plans, it would then be necessary to have available only the master file, rather than the bulky case folders. You need to develop an efficient strategy to meet your individual clinical needs.

H. Each spring or fall, IEPs are constructed for students. The short–term objectives listed and met in October, for example, might be at, above or below the criterion level by the end of the academic year. It is important to take time, therefore, at the end of the year, to do some review testing of short–term IEP objectives (see Appendix 14). Sequence all short–term objectives from September through May. If a student has progressed in articulation therapy, for example, from syllable level to use of the sound in words or sentences, test for the use of the sound at the highest level of proficiency reached. If, however, a student has reached 90 to 100 percent accuracy in drill on copular *is* and 60 percent accuracy when copular *is* appears in spontaneous usage, it is recommended that both the drill and spontaneous levels be checked. As a general guideline, any behavior that is still being stabilized should be reviewed at a variety of levels to evaluate the present level of competence (see Appendix 14).

NOTE: It is not suggested that *all* evaluation strategies described be instituted prior to therapy. Collect data *during* therapy. Accumulate sufficient baseline data that will allow you to initiate therapy and then refine your evaluative data over time. The author rarely does more than the following during the initial evaluation: a language sample of approximately 40 to 75 utterances, PPVT, Grammatic Closure Subtest, CELI and the TACL or Test of Linguistic Concepts. The entire evaluation and analysis of data per child should not take more than 2½ hours.

Test References for Appendix 4

Before We Read
H. M. Robinson, M. Monroe and A. S. Artley
Scott, Foresman and Company (1962)

Peabody Picture Vocabulary Test
Lloyd M. Dunn
American Guidance Service, Inc.
Publishers' Building
Circle Pines, Minnesota 55014

Deep Test of Articulation
Eugene McDonald
Stanwix House, Inc.
3020 Chartiers Ave.
Pittsburgh, Pennsylvania 15204

Grammatic Closure Subtest
Illinois Test of Psycholinguistic Abilities (ITPA)
S. A. Kirk, J. J. McCarthy and W. D. Kirk
University of Illinois Press
Urbana, Illinois 61801

Carrow Elicited Language Inventory (CELI)
Elizabeth Carrow-Woolfolk
Teaching Resources
100 Boylston Street
Boston, Massachusetts 02116

Test for Auditory Comprehension of Language (TACL)
Elizabeth Carrow-Woolfolk
Teaching Resources
100 Boylston Street
Boston, Massachusetts 02116

Environmental Language Inventory (ELI)
James D. MacDonald
Charles E. Merrill Publishing Co.
A Bell and Howell Company
Columbus, Ohio 43216

Boehm Test of Basic Concepts (BTBC)
Ann Boehm
Psychological Corporation
304 East 45th St.
New York, New York 10017

Assessment of Children's Language Comprehension (ACLC)
R. Foster, J. Giddan and J. Stark
Consulting Psychologists Press, Inc.
577 College Avenue
Palo Alto, California 93406

In Other Words
A. Schiller and W. A. Jenkins
Scott, Foresman and Company
Glenview, Illinois

My Life Pictionary – Multiple Meaning Words
Instructional Industries, Inc.
Executive Park
Ballston Lake, New York 12019

Language Remediation and Expansion – 100 Skill Building Reference Lists
Communication Skill Builders, Inc.
Post Office Box 42050
Tucson, Arizona 85733

California Test of Mental Maturity (CTMM)
E. T. Sullivan, L. W. Clar and E. W. Tiegs
Monterey Test Bureau
Monterey, California

Test of Linguistic Concepts
E. H. Wiig and E. M. Semel
In *Language Disabilities in Children and Adolescents*
Charles E. Merrill Publishing Company
Columbus, Ohio 43216

Utah Test of Language Development
M. J. Mecham, J. Lurin Jex and J. Jones
Communication Research Associates, Inc.
Post Office Box 11012
Salt Lake City, Utah 84111

APPENDIX 5
Looking for Deficient Patterns in a Language Sample

The purpose of obtaining a language sample is to get an estimate of how competent/incompetent a speaker appears to his listener. When transcribing the sample from the tape, make notations on deficient patterns. For specific suggestions on how to probe pertinent behaviors, consult Appendix 4. In addition, see Section IV of the monograph, which provides examples of various incompetent communication behaviors and should, therefore, reflect more completely on the types of patterns the clinician should consider. The following examples demonstrate a few ways in which the author makes notations on ineffective and incompetent patterns in the language sample transcript. The percentage of occurrence of each major pattern is calculated and this figure acts as the baseline for remediation and future evaluation of programming effectiveness.

I. Syntactic

Key: ✓ restricted sentence
      ★ correct use of a commonly restricted form
      ∧ missing form
      ○ substituted form

Case: J. K., age 9 (6.13 MLU)

MLU (words):

2 ✓ 1.   What∧ this?

3 ✓ 2.   Here ∧my pass.

4 ✓ 3.   (Her) wa∧ watching TV.

5 ✓ 4.   (Her) (get) *goes/went* in the kitchen.

8 ✓ 5.   When (her) got back, the crackers <u>was</u> gone. *were*

7   6.   The dog was sitting beside the chair.

9 ✓ 7.   (Her) walked∧ *to* get a dust pan and a broom.

4 ✓ 8. ★ <u>She</u> drop∧ her books.

9 ✓ 9. ∧ Pick∧ em up and put em in [<u>this thing</u>]. *egocentric imprecise vocabulary*

The *complete sample* (of 79 sentences) for this case showed the following major patterns:

1. 54 percent of the sentences were restricted (showed one or more grammatical errors).

2. Major causes of the 54 percent restricted sentences were (and there might have been more than one reason per sentence):
   a. 29 percent — omission of the auxiliary
   b. 29 percent — omission of - -*ed* tense marker
   c. 44 percent — objective for subjective pronoun usage

3. Sentence complexity indicated:
   a. simple — 41/79 (52 percent)
   b. simple sentence plus prepositional phrase — 14/79 (18 percent)
   c. compound — 11/79 (14 percent)
   d. complex — 6/79 (8 percent)
   e. combinations of the above — 7/79 (9 percent)

II. Intelligibility

Case: A. C., age 9 (6.72 MLU)

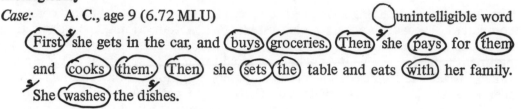

The *complete sample* of 32 sentences showed that 31 percent of the words were unintelligible (with the criterion being that the clinician had to replay the tape two or more times to discern the word being uttered).

III. Giant Words

Case: G. R., age 10 (9.71 MLU)   ⌐⌐ giant word complex

GW	W	
0	6	1. A vase is for holding flowers.
2	5	2. It ˌgives–you–nice–beauty.ˌ
3	4	3. ˌThis–isˌ a bib.
7	10	4. It keeps ˌthe–babyˌ ˌfrom–spillingˌ some stuff ˌon–it.ˌ
6	8	5. ˌA–shoestringˌ is to put ˌin–yourˌ shoe.

The *complete sample* indicated that when this student spoke at a rate of 84 words per minute, only 10 percent of his words were unintelligible. However, when he spoke at 170 words per minute, 38 percent of his words were unintelligible. He reduced his number of "giant words" when he decreased his speech rate. If his MLU were calculated in terms of the number of words per sentence his listener heard, the figure was 8.1 (as compared to the actual 9.71 MLU). See Section IV, example 8, for further details on "giant words."

IV. Verbal Mazes

Case: D. W., age 11 (10.85 MLU)   M = Maze in sentence
                                          [ ] = Words in the verbal maze

Mazes:

1	1.	M The shoestring [goes in the] goes in the holes in the shoe.
	2.	It keeps your shoe tight.
	3.	A saddle goes on a horse.
1	4.	M Ya gotta tighten up the saddle [so you] so the saddle won't fall off.
3	5.	M The stamp [the stamp] goes on the [goes on the] envelope [on the envelope] on the right side.

The *complete sample* showed 14/28 (50 percent) of the sentences having verbal mazes. There was an average of 1.5 verbal mazes in these fourteen sentences. (See Section IV, example 7, for further details on verbal mazing.)

APPENDIX 6
Competence Versus Performance —
Probing for a Gap Between the Two

It is important to distinguish between linguistic habits, as shown in spontaneous language usage, and the linguistic knowledge that the individual possesses. Sentence imitation or modeling of story details can frequently shed light upon the gap between an individual's language performance and his true competence.

I. **Difference in Sampling Conditions** (Case S. C.)

  A. Peer dialogue

      This is my thing.   No, I'm playing with these.   Get over here.   You can't come up here.   I'm making a play.

  B. Telling a story in response to sequential pictures

      The girl looked down and the dog looked up at her. The dog saw the potato chips on the floor. The girl went somewhere. When she got back she said, "That dog has eaten the potato chips." The doggie ate it all.

II. **Difference in Performance Conditions** (Case J. J.)

  A. Spontaneous storytelling

      He's dipping the paint in. He has a helmet on. He starts painting. He looks up and paint drips in his face. He wipes it off. He takes the helmet off and he gives it to his dad.

  B. Therapist provides a model prior to storytelling

      Jim was playing spaceman. He came around the corner and was watching his dad paint. The paint dripped down from the paint brush and into his face. His dad was wiping off the paint on his face. He said, "Here Dad, put this on." He did and the paint dripped down on the helmet and not his face.

III. **Performance Reflects Memory Deficit and Syntactic/Semantic Deficiencies**
  (Case P. M.)

  A. Spontaneous storytelling

      Once pon a time was a girl named Cinderella. Mean little step mothers told her to wash the clothes. She did. Then she got married. She got locked in her room. Body got the key and locked her out. The next morning they got married.

  B. Storytelling after a model presentation of the fairy tale

      She had a mean stepmother and a mean stepsister. The stepsister went to the palace. Fairy godmother told her, "get married." She did at twelve o'clock. The prince found Cinderella. They live happily after.

Hannah Linguistic Summary Sheet*

USING THE HANNAH LINGUISTIC SUMMARY SHEET

1. Transcribe the language sample.

2. While structures used are still fresh in your mind, fill out the Summary Sheet. You can complete much of the Summary Sheet from memory. For example, you will undoubtedly remember whether the child used a *proper noun* and whether this structure was used two times or more during a fifty-word utterance sample. If it has been, place two check marks (✓).

3. Research has shown that if a child uses a structure two or more times within a fifty-word utterance sample, it may be assumed that he has that structure within his linguistic rule system. This is not to say that the rule appears consistently, however.

4. If a child uses a structure at least twice within his fifty-word utterance sample, but also shows substitutions or omissions of that structure, mark "inc." signaling that use of the structure is inconsistent.

5. If you have evaluated a particular structure in elicited imitation or on some other test but have not gotten it within the language sample, make these notes on the form (such as "no–GC," meaning irregular plural nouns were in error on the *ITPA* Grammatic Closure subtest).

6. Note the general transformational level at which the child is functioning. Include some of the structures he currently is not using as IEP goals.

7. Hannah has provided some developmental norms in her book which can be used if you wish and examples of each transformational rule are provided.

8. Calculate the number of utterances that were: fragments, simple, compound, complex, simple plus prepositional phrase.

---

*Reproduced with the permission of the author and publisher from *Applied Linguistic Analysis, II* (1977), Elaine P. Hannah, SenCom Associates, P.O. Box 36, Pacific Palisades, CA 90272.

(See page 114 for sample Summary Sheet.)

HANNAH LINGUISTIC SUMMARY SHEET

Name _S.C._   Age _8.7_   Examiner _Simon_

Address _____   Telephone_____   B.D. _11-10-73_   Date _5-8-81_

Type of Sample: 15 utt____   50+____   50- _✓(40)_   Ps____

PERIOD I: Emerging Language Patterns

	No.	%		No.	%
One Word Units			Three Word Units		
Two Word Units			Basal Sentences		

PERIOD II: Common Syntactic Patterns (three years +)

Count N	✓	Tense irreg past	✓ inc.	T – contr	✓✓
Proper N	✓✓	V + ing	✓✓	T – neg	✓✓
N pl affix	✓	B + V + ing	✓✓	T – do	✓ inc.
Def art seg } inc.	✓✓	V + NP	✓✓	T – coord	✓✓
Indef art seg	✓✓	V + participle	✓✓	T – pronom	
Dem Seg	✓✓	V + adv (-ly = inc.)	✓	T – V compl inf	con. er.
Pron number - s	✓✓	V + prep phrase	✓✓	T – wh Q	✓✓
Pron number - p	✓✓	Copula + NP	✓✓	T – pron	✓✓
Pron subj	✓✓	Copula + prep phrase	✓	T – adj	✓
Pron obj	✓✓	Modal	✓✓	T – y/n Q	✓
Pron masc	✓✓	Inf marker seg	✓ inc.	T – conj del	✓
Pron fem	✓✓	Modifier	✓✓	T – poss	✓✓
Tense pres affix	✓✓ inc.				

PERIOD II: Less Commonly Used Syntactic Patterns

Indef pron seg	✓	T – compar ⌈GC - regular erfest - OK		T – N compl	✓
Copula + adj	✓✓	T – imper ⌊irreg. - no		T – reflex	no – GC
Copula + adv (-ly inc.)	✓	T – got	✓	T – conj	
Sentential adv		T – ellipsis	✓✓	T – rel	no – CELI
Intensifier		T – inversion		T – rel red	
N pl irreg	no – GC	T – V compl N cl		T – tag Q	OK – CELI
V + adj	✓	T – subord	✓	T – nominaliz	
Have + V + ed	no – GC	T – pass	OK – CELI	T – appos	
Mass N	✓	T – pass del		T – cleft	
Tense reg past	✓✓	T – indir obj		T – extrapos	
T – there	✓	T – indir obj del		T – recip	
T – participle shift	OK – CELI	T – V compl part			

NOTES

① MLU
   a. 6.76 - Sequential picture description
   b. 4.36 - playing cars with a peer

② uses _that_ frequently in preference to articles

③ Sentence Complexity (37 statements)
   a. fragment + 1/39 (3%)
   b. simple ++++++++++++++++++++++++++ 24/37 (65%)
   c. simple + prep. phrase +++++++ 7/37 (19%)
   d. compound +++++ 5/37 (14%)
   e. complex 0

④ Questions
   a. Yes/no +
   b. Wh ++

KEY TO NOTATIONS:
*GC refers to performance on the Grammatic Closure (ITPA) Subtest.

*inc. comments that while this form appeared twice, it was sometimes in error, and therefore development was inconsistent.

*con. er. means that the form was consistently in error.

*OK CELI means that while this form did not appear in the language sample, it was elicited on the CELI.

APPENDIX 8
Simon Clinician Worksheet

NAME: C. H.   Age: 8.0   BD: 1-2-73   TEACHER: S. V.   DATE: 1-17-81

Reason for Referral

"immature speech"

	Relevant Tests

General Observations

① Response style - on PPVT, made an impulsive first choice, reconsidered & chose a second, generally correct, picture

② Enjoys communication; conversational

Utah 5.0 ma

Phonology

① Immature (reduced) later blends

② Errors on /s/, /ʃ/, /θ/, /ʒ/, /v/

} primary contributors to "immature speech" image and reduced intelligibility

	I	M	F

Morphology

① Receptively (TACL)
  a. doesn't comprehend significance of -s 3rd person singular
  b. OK on derivational markers

② Expressively
  a. 3rd person -s: 00000000000+00 -14/15 (93% error)
  b. -ed past tense: 0++0+0++0+0++0+ -6/15 (40% error)

Grammatic Closure 5.0 ma

Syntax - 44/16 (61%) restricted sentences

① 4.77 MLU
② Receptive Errors (TACL)
  a. s/θ distinctions
  b. semantics of wh-question words
  c. has/have number distinctions
  d. will as a future tense marker
  e. gender distinction in pronouns
③ Expressive Errors (sample)
  a. she (her/she): +0000000+0000 -11/13 (85% error)
  b. copular is/was: 0000+0++000+0 -9/13 (69% error)
  c. auxiliary is/was: 0000+++++0000+ -7/13 (58% error)

TACL 6.7 ma

CELI (9-78)
83% of the sentences showed errors
a. inflectional markers
b. reduction of compound verbs
c. inconsistent her/she
d. omission - relative clause

Semantics

① On PPVT - missed transportation & appliance → probe understanding of superordinate/subordinate relationships

② On basis of TACL responses - knowledge of Boehm concepts should be evaluated.

PPVT (A) 5.7 ma

Interpersonal Communication

① Generally:
  a. Considerable "mumbling" during storytelling as if it's not important for the listener to hear all of the details
  b. tends to restate rather than clarify an unclear message
② Functions:
  a. imaginative: good, creative story-line when playing with boys, but cannot say a nursery rhyme or tell a familiar fairy tale (Utah).
  b. interactional: dialogue is appropriate to topic.
  c. heuristic: asks questions when he doesn't understand a task and also to find out about the school and clinician.
  d. representational: observes details in a sequential picture story and clearly relates them; personal experiences related - lack details

115

SIMON CLINICIAN WORKSHEET

Student: S. C. Date: 5-15-81
Birthdate: 10-26-71 Age: 7.7
Teacher: M. H. Room: 105

Referral source and reason: Classroom teacher referred him because "he has immature language and doesn't understand what is said to him."

General Observations:
Slow formulation (or speech) rate — 70 words per minute
Has difficulty reconstructing sentence structures in an Interactive
  Language Teaching lesson
MLU: 6.76 on picture description; 4.36 on peer interaction

	Relevant Tests		
Phonology	**I**	**M**	**F**
–substitutions	f/θ	f/θ	f/θ
–confuses, reverses, omits and adds sounds in words		s/ʃ	s/ʃ
(balanya/banana)		d/ʒ	d/ʒ
–error phonemes are above age 4			

Morphology	
–3rd person singluar –s omitted 18 percent of time –consistent omission of –ly on adverbs –total inflection omission (100 sentences) 4 percent of time	Gr. Clos. — ITPA 5.0 MA (severe) tense, number

Syntax	
–uses *that* in preference to articles (a, the) –60 percent of irregular plural nouns in error –65 percent of irregular past tense verbs in error –70 percent of infinitive "to" missing –37 percent of 42 compound sentences the tense was changed in the middle of the sentence –unsure of reflexive pronouns, with exception of "myself" –36 percent of 100 sentences showed restrictions –35 percent of longer (compound and complex) sentences showed mazes	NSST: 33% errors — R 72% errors — E CELI: 82% of sentences showed some error

Semantics	
–unsure of spatial (in, on, beside) and structural (to, at, for) prepositions –receptive vocabulary is 2 years below age level (most errors were nouns; superordinate titles and synonyms for more basic vocabulary) –auditory constraints limit his ability to process meaningful inflections on words and series of words in sentences –knows primary colors	PPVT: 5.1 MA signal, capsule, transportation Utah Test of Lang. Devel.: 5.0 MA

Interpersonal Communication
Dialogue: cannot stay on topic; does not address himself to the semantics of Wh-
  questions (gives a "what" answer to a "why" question)
Functions: interpersonal — aggressive; regulatory — instructions are egocentric;
  representational — cannot sequence details coherently; imaginative — cannot
  tell a fairy tale or nursery rhyme or construct a story involving toys

Name: R. T.   Age: 12   BD: 5-10-69   Teacher: A. N.   Date: 5-7-81

Reason for Referral
"He has difficulty expressing himself."
"He scored low on the ITPA Grammatic Closure Subtest."

General Observations:
Voice is rather high-pitched and the inflection pattern is static.
In therapy — responds well to drill (i.e., dramatic gains on the
the GC Subtest.

	Relevant Tests		
Phonology	I	M	F
1. Articulation — OK			
2. "Giant words" appeared in 8/62 sentences (13%)			

Morphology
1. —ed +O++++++++O   –2/12 missing 17% of the time
2. —ing ++++++++++OO+++ –2/15 missing 13% of the time

Relevant Tests: Grammatic Closure (5/81) 9.2 ma 28/33 (compared to 5.2 in 5–80)

Syntax
1. MLU 7.24 (62 sentences)
2. –18/62 (29%) restricted sentences caused by:
   a. omission of forms 5/18 (28%)
   b. word substitutions 4/18 (22%)
   c. semantically confusing statements 5/18 (28%)
   d. combination of above factors 3/18 (17%)
   e. count noun/article disagreement 1/18 (5%)
3. consistent tense reference in sequential stories
   O+OO+OO   –5/7 (71% error rate)
4. performance/competence gap
   a. spontaneous MLU 7.6/post–model MLU 7.1
   b. spontaneous MLU 8.5/post–model MLU 9.0
      MLU not improved as much as degree of coherence

Relevant Tests: TACL (12–80) 6.4 ma

Semantics
1. Semantically confusing statements/questions
   ++++++ 6/62 (10%)
2. inappropriate vocabulary choices (was/came; onto/into)

Relevant Tests: ACLC (5–81) B – 100% C – 100% D – 100% PPVT (12–80) 6.6 ma

Interpersonal Communication
1. sentences with verbal mazes (of 2+ words per maze) — 13/62 (21%)
   a. 6/13 (46%) — one maze per sentence
   b. 6/13 (46%) — two mazes per sentence
   c. average number of words per maze 2.95
2. Representational function O+O++ –2/5 (40%) content unclear without
   sequential pictures

(Continued on page 118)

Interpersonal Communication (continued)
3. Interactional (dialogue) o+++++ooo+ooo+ –7/14 (50% of interactional comments were unproductive
4. Heuristic function
    a. questions +ooo –3/4 (75%) were unproductive
    b. explanations oo+o –3/4 (75%) were incoherent

Using the Clinician Worksheet

1. Transcribe the language sample.

2. Put a check (✓) next to any restricted sentence and an **M** next to any sentence that has a verbal maze and bracket giant words. See Appendix 9.

3. Complete the Hannah Linguistic Summary Sheet (to indicate the structures upon which the child relies for construction of messages).

4. Note error patterns on the worksheet that are most responsible for the child's appearing incompetent in his use of language structure in the appropriate section. (See sections on morphology and syntax on the sample Clinician Worksheet for examples of dominant patterns noted and Appendix 5.)

5. Return to the sample and count the obligatory contexts in which the structure appears or does not appear. (Place a plus (+) each time it appears and a zero (o) each time it does not appear. You will find, with a little practice, that you will be able to scan the sample for several error forms simultaneously, putting the o or the + next to each of the error forms you find. Place the total number of errors above the number of obligatory contexts and calculate the percentage of times the structure is in error.

6. Calculate percentage of occurrence for any feature that contributes to the child's profile as an incompetent communicator; number of sentences characterized by giant words, number of restricted sentences, number of sentences with verbal mazes and all structural errors.

7. Make notes on any of Halliday's language functions evaluated under Interpersonal Communication.

8. Insert pertinent scores from tests in the right–hand column.

APPENDIX 9
An Example of a Language Sample Scenario, Transcription and Analysis

KEY:

C	not included in MLU	⌐⌐	words run together into a "giant word" (see Section IV, example 8)
>	clinician comments	M	verbal maze in sentence
✓	restricted sentence	[ ]	words within maze
⊘	substituted form		
sem.	semantically restricted	∧	omitted form

Case: R. T., age 12 (7.24 MLU)

There are four pictures in this story: 1-2-3-4 (pointing to the sequential order). You tell me the story.

MLU
(words)

11   1.   She· [she] had some [potatoes] potato chips in a plate on the stool.

6   2. M   She spilt em on the floor [they fell∧on-the-floor] [on the floor.]

4   3.   The dog's right there.

sem. 13 ✓ 4.   The dog start∧ta eat em up and then the plate's all gone. *(semantically confusing)*

4   5.   She's cleaning it up. *(Split tense reference in story.)*

Good. I'm going to tell you my story about these pictures and then we're going to play copy cat. I want you to tell me my story back. Are you ready?

One day Sue was watching a cowboy movie on TV. She was hungry, so she had a bowl of potato chips. She reached for a potato chip and the whole bowl fell on the floor, right next to her dog, Spot. She thought, "Oh, oh, I'd better clean up this mess," so she went out to the kitchen to get a dust pan and brush. While she was gone, Spot started eating the potato chips and by the time she got back, the potato chips were all gone. Spot had eaten every one of them.

Okay, you tell me my story back.

6   6.   One day Sue was watching TV.

3   7.   She was hungry.

12 ✓ 8. M   She reached for a [eat a] potato chips *(number disagreement)* and she reached for-another-one.

6   9.   The bowl fell on the floor.

10 ✓ 10.   By the time she (was) *came/got* back, they were all gone.

6 ✓ 11.   Spot (has) *had* all eaten∧em *of* up.

>Good. Tell me this story.

17   12. M   One day _she-was_ pickin up books and _she-was-trying_ [ta put in a] [she's trying] ta get em up into there.

13   13.   She's _puttin-em-into_ a <u>dish thing</u> where you put plates and forks in.   *labeling restriction*   *1 word*

4   14.   She's carrying the books. *(Split tense reference in story.)*

>Good. Tell me this story.

5   15. M   He [he fell] fell [she fell] on the floor [stuff fell on the floor].

7   16.   The boy tried to pick it up.

7✓ 17.   _They-hadda-vacuum_ and a girl (come). *Came*

sem. 15   18.   She tried ta vacuum the boy but it was stuff mother tried to do that.

>Good. We're going to play copy–cat again. Remember, listen to my story about these pictures and then tell me my story.

One day Tom and Jane decided to make a cake. Jane said, "Tom, please get the flour." Tom reached for the flour and when he did, it fell all over his shirt and pants and the floor. Jane said, "Oh, no, look at the mess you've made." She tried to brush him off and then she called to Mother, who was in the next room vacuuming. She said, "Mom, we made a mess in here. Could you help us?" Mom came in and vacuumed Tom off and then she vacuumed the floor.

You tell me my story now.

13   19.   One day Tom was gonna make a cake∧to reach for the flour. *(and he needed)*

13   20. M   When he did, [it] it [went all over the place] went all over his shirt, pants and the floor.

6   21.   The little girl said "Oh, no."

4   22.   It was all over.

10   23.   The little girl called for Mom _in-the-other-room._

10   24.   Help! We made a mess and we need your help [. . . and the floor.]

7   25.   Mother vacuumed up Tommy and the floor.

>Good. I have some pictures about a little girl. She goes through the same routine every morning. Tell me what she does each morning.

5   26.   She wakes up every morning.

5   27.   She takes her pajamas off.

4   28.   She has her clothes.

4   29.   She eats her breakfast.

5   30.   She gets on the bus.

4 31. She walks into school.

4 32. She's in school working. *(Change of tense)*

>Good. This next story is about a boy who has an accident. This accident happened last Saturday. I want you to tell me what happened last Saturday.

8 33. One Saturday the boy was riding a bicycle.

7 34. [She] he saw-a-log and went "Oh."

4 35. [She] (then) he fell and cried.

2 36. M He's crying [tear tear] [and a sore leg.] *(Change of tense)*

5 ✓ 37. He came to (her) his mother.

4 ✓ 38. He Got a sore leg.

4 39. Now she's bandaging it. *(Change of tense)*

>Good. I'd like for you to be the teacher now. Explain to me how these things go together. How do these two things go together?

Needle/thread

7 ✓ 40. You put the thread (onto) into the needle.

sem. *9* ✓ 41. M You probably tie it on and [you sew the thread] — [up his pants] — you sew things.

Skillet/stove *(Relationship not really explained.)*

5 ✓ 42. It Fry pan goes on stove.

6 43. It heats up and gets hot.

Paint/paintbrush

8 44. M There's paint there and there's a paint brush — [those two.]

13 45. M The paint brush is [to paint] to go in the paint and paint the wall.

Baby/bib

sem. ✓ 46. M Cause — on the baby — cause that's a bib — cause when you slop — the bib is the slop on the baby — it's the slop on — when you slop *(non-productive sentence with multiple images)*

Hangar/coat

14 47. Cause the hanger is for the shirt and you hang it up in the closet.

7 48. M [Hang it up on the little bar thing] — [round thing] — you hang it up in the closet.

>Why do you do that? *(Why question not answered.)*

sem. *11* ✓ 49. (Cause) there's a thing right there where ya hang em on with.

>Why do you hang up your coat?

6 50. So you'll know where it is.

>Tell me about your summer. What will you be doing this summer?

1 ✓ 51. ∧Go∧for a Y–program and go∧swimming. *(I am / ing to / my)*

8 52. They have a lot of swimming lessons there.

12 53. They'll do arts and crafts, and then after that is the zoo.

11 54. ,We-learn,all about the animals and do arts and crafts.

10 55. I haven't played with that car in a long time [with the magnet.]

>What would you like to do? How could you ask me to use it? *(processed a why question)*

9 ✓ 56. (Cause) I haven't play∧with it in a long time. *(ed)*

>I know. How could you ask me to use it?

1 57. Yeah.

>Ask me if you may use it. Can you ask me?

6 58. (Yeah) . . . May I use that thing please?
(He is playing with the magnetic car toy.)

sem. ✓ 59. What will happen if you do keep on doing it with touching the thing? *(non-productive question)*

>Excuse me? I don't understand.

11 60. M [How come the most thing] how come you have to do it without touching the thing?

>What do you mean?

10 ✓ 61. When you move the little steel thing around in her — this. *(up?)*

>Do you mean, why do you need the magnet to move the car?

1 62. (Yeah.) Why?

Comments on the Case

Whenever the clinician looks at a language sample transcript, the question should be posed, "How can I 'milk' this to give me any data available on incompetent communication skills?"

This case was included in the Appendix because it presents an opportunity to view a transcription of a 12–year–old clinical case who does not have an inordinate number of syntactic and morphological problems. Nevertheless, he is an incompetent communicator, and data need to be gathered that demonstrate *why* he appears incompetent to the listener.

The reader will notice that a separate "giant word" MLU (see Section IV, example 8) was not tabulated for this boy. The author uses the guideline of 20 percent or more sentences with "giant words" to determine whether or not a separate "giant word" MLU is tabulated. Secondly, it can be noted that while all words spoken are transcribed, those in verbal mazes are not counted in the MLU. In every instance, the speaker is given the benefit of the doubt when deciding what is part of the final message and what has been lost in confusion (or verbal mazes). For example, note utterance 20.

Finally, when the author presents a "model story," this is not transcribed. Instead, the word "model" is placed on the line above the student's post–model story.

This boy's major difficulty seems to be that he cannot code his perceptions and thoughts coherently at all times. His thoughts frequently seem to be more complex than his structural skills permit him to code. This gap results in semantically confusing statements and questions. He would profit from a reduced MLU composed of coherent and semantically appropriate word combinations, as well as attention to the details presented to him in directions and dialogue (i.e., auditory processing skill development.). In other words, the major components of his programming should be functional (as contrasted to structural) at this time. It is more important that he reduce his 28 percent semantically confusing statements than it is for him to reduce his 17 percent omission of the —ed past tense marker. In addition, he needs to develop subordination skills so he can readily construct meaningful and efficient complex sentences. See Appendix 8, example C, for R. T.'s "Needs Profile."

APPENDIX 10
A Longitudinal Evaluation Summary

NAME: S. K. BD: 11-15-69 Entered Therapy: 9-77

S = spontaneous
D = Drill

Tests

dates of evaluations	PPVT (A) (receptive vocabulary)	Grammatic Closure Subtest	TACL (auditory comp. of language)	CELI (elicited imitation)	Utah (developmental language)	ACLC (comp. of critical elements)	DAI (articulation)
9-77	5.1 ma	5.0 ma +1/33 69% error	4.8 ma +70/101 30% error	+10/52 81% error	5.0 ma	—	20 errors
5-78	—	6.8 ma +20/33 39% error	5.9 ma +80/101 20% error	+24/52 54% error	—	B. 90% C. 70% D. 50% correct	11 errors
5-79	8.1 ma	8.10 ma +27/33 18% error	6.11 ma +96/101 5% error	+46/52 12% error	7.7 ma	B. 100% C. 100% D. 90% correct	4 errors

Sample Notations

dates	MLU (mean length of utterance)	Omission of Subject D	Omission of Subject S	Substitution of her/she D	Substitution of her/she S	Irregular past tense verb errors D	Irregular past tense verb errors S	Omission of copular is/was D	Omission of copular is/was S	Omission of auxiliary is/was D	Omission of auxiliary is/was S	Omission of 3rd person singular –s D	Omission of 3rd person singular –s S	Omission of infinitive to D	Omission of infinitive to S	Number of sentences with verbal mazes of 2+ words per image D	Number of sentences with verbal mazes of 2+ words per image S	Percentage of restricted sentences in sample
9-77	5.24 24 ant.	—	-11/24 46%	—	-4/4 100%	—	-2/3 67%	—	-4/9 67%	—	-5/5 100%	—	-2/2 100%	—	-4/4 100%	—	-9/24 38%	-18/24 54%
5-78	6.76 50 ant.	—	-16/50 32%	-2/10 20%	-4/11 34%	-1/10 10%	-3/12 25%	-3/10 30%	-3/8 27%	-2/10 20%	-4/11 36%	-0/10 0%	-2/13 15%	-1/10 10%	-3/11 27%	-1/10 10%	-3/50 16%	-19/50 38%
5-79	7.64 58 ant.	—	-4/58 10%	-0/10 0%	-1/16 6%	0/10 0%	-5/28 18%	-0/10 0%	-1/10 0%	-0/10 0%	-2/12 16%	-0/10 0%	1/9 1%	-0/10 0%	-0/8 0%	-0/10 0%	-4/58 7%	-9/58 16%

See note to Appendix 10 on next page.

NOTE: Under "Tests," is is recommended that you quote scores in terms of what you feel gives you the most graphic gross indication of progress. For a more analytical impression, your notes on the test protocol can be consulted. As an example, you will note on the CELI that the author quotes percentage of sentences that showed errors instead of percentiles. This is a gross indicator that has proven to be more revealing than the percentile rankings offered in the test because many students in my caseload are bove 7–11 CA, the top of the normative data. In addition, it is recommended that when data are based on 50 or fewer responses or cover a limited age range, you include a fractional figure representing the number of responses correct (or incorrect, if you prefer) out of the total number of responses on that test. For example, under "Grammatic Closure" (5–79), +27/33 indicates that only 6 items on the test were missed.

Under the Sample Notations, the fractional numbers indicate the number of times the error occurred in its obligatory context. For example, during the 5–79 evaluation, there were 58 utterances analyzed. Each utterance has an obligatory context for a *subject,* so the fraction –6/58 indicates that in six sentences, no subject appeared. Under *irregular past tense verbs* the fraction –5/28 indicates that there were twenty–eight obligatory contexts for irregular past tense verbs, but in five contexts the student did not make an appropriate conjugation. For example, he may have said "builded" or just said the base verb "run" instead of conjugating it to "ran."

APPENDIX 11
Loban's Oral Language Scale*

1. Skill in communication	no awareness of listeners; speaks without any effort to evoke understanding from others; pace of words and inflection of voice not adjusted to listeners	1 2 3 4 5	adjusts pace of and inflection to listener; uses an "imparting tone"; is aware of need to make self understood
2. Organization, purpose, and control	rambles; no sense of order or of getting to the point; rattles on without purpose; cannot tell a story in proper sequence	1 2 3 4 5	plans what is said; gets to the point; *controls* language; can tell a story in proper sequence
3. Wealth of ideas	never expresses an idea; appears dull and unimaginative; doesn't originate suggestions or plans during play periods	1 2 3 4 5	expresses ideas on different topics; makes suggestions on what to do and how to carry out class plans; shows imagination and creativity in play
4. *Amount* of language (regardless of quality of language)	seldom talks; exceptionally quiet; needs to be prompted to talk	1 2 3 4 5	talks freely, frequently and easily; talks about all the time, if permitted
5. Vocabulary	uses a meager vocabulary, far below that of most children this age; inarticulate; mute	1 2 3 4 5	uses a rich variety of words; has an exceptionally large and growing vocabulary; speaks fluently
6. Quality of listening	inattentive; easily distracted; seldom attends to the spoken language of others	1 2 3 4 5	superior attentiveness and understanding of spoken language
7. Quality of	omissions of structural elements, including word endings; uses only simple, active, declarative sentences; word order difficulties in question formations	1 2 3 4 5	includes all structural elements; mature sentence patterns; maintains constant tense reference within a paragraph or story; mature use of phrases and clauses and conjunctions

*Loban, W. *Language Ability in the Middle-Grades of Elementary School.* U.S. Office of Education (1961).

APPENDIX 12
Sequencing Programming Objectives

NAME: S. C.   TEACHER: G. W.   ROOM: 1   SCHOOL: DDS   DATE: 9–77/5–78

Program Components	IEP Notations
Phonology 1. auditory sequencing of sounds 2. production of /θ/ and /ð/	1. By using teacher–constructed drill materials, S. will be able to produce a series of three CV combinations (tha, thee, tho) at speech speed with 90 percent accuracy by 11-1-78.
Morphology 1. –ed past tense marker 2. 3rd person singular marker 3. –ly adverbial marker	1. By using teacher–constructed drill materials, S. will produce the third person singular –s and past tense –ed markers with 80 percent accuracy by 11-15-78.
Syntax 1. use of articles 2. question (wh) formation 3. Irregular past tense verbs 4. gots/has clarification 5. inclusion of infinitive marker 6. reflexive pronouns 7. use of multiple auxiliaries	Long–Term: S. will evidence no more than 25 percent restricted sentences within a fifty–sentence sample by 5-15-79. 1. By using teacher–constructed drill materials, S. will supply the infinitive marker "to" with 60 percent accuracy in sentences without infinitive complement by 12-15-78.
Semantics 1. semantic value of prepositions 2. "mine" vs. "my" clarification 3. vocabulary building	1. By using commercial flashcards, S. will be able to correctly identify the spatial placement of people and objects through the use of prepositions by 12-15-77.
Interpersonal Communication 1. recite a nursery rhyme 2. provide the sequential events in his morning schedule 3. explain the functional relationship between two objects	1. By using the Walt Disney Story Books, S. will choose a nursery rhyme and be able to recite it by 12-15-77.

APPENDIX 13
Sample Short-Term IEP Objectives*

I. Emerging Language

1. Using CC* Agent/Action photos, J. will be able to provide agent/action constructions in drill with 80 percent accuracy by _____.

2. Using a flannel board fairy tale, K. will be able to formulate agent/action/object, X/locative and modifier/head constructions within an interactive teaching format with 90 percent accuracy by _____.

3. Using CC sequential filmstrip stories, J. will be able to provide a description of actions pictured using two- to three-word utterances by _____.

II. Cracking the Code

1. Using the CC verb drill cards, J. will be able to conjugate and use in drill sentences twenty irregular past tense verbs by _____.

2. Using CC agent/action and action/object photo cards, J. will be able to provide —ed past tense markers for all regular verbs by _____.

3. Using CC agent/action photo cards, M. will be able to produce the infinitive *to* (without complement) in drill with 80 percent accuracy by _____.

4. Using CC X/location photo cards, S. will be able to formulate "Where is the _____ ?" questions with 80 percent accuracy by _____.

III. Marginal Communicators

1. Using CC occupation/profession photo cards, H. will be able to sufficiently organize his thoughts prior to speaking so that no more than 20 percent of his sentences describing the occupations show mazing.

2. Using CC sequential filmstrip stories, N. will be able to tell a story in past, present, or future tense upon clinician request by _____.

3. Using CC regulatory function cards, R. will be able to explain, in an audible voice, the playing rules for two board games by _____.

IV. Language Different

1. E. will be able to transcribe five Black English sentences into standard English within a fifteen-minute period by _____.

2. M. will be able to evaluate an incomplete task request made by the clinician and ask sufficient questions to clarify the instructions by _____.

---

*Simon, C. S. *Communicative Competence: A Functional-Pragmatic Language Program.* Tucson: Communication Skill Builders, 1980.

IEP Review Checklist

Name: *E.C.* Age: *9.8* Teacher: *M.L.* Date: *5-30-79*

ORIGINAL OBJECTIVES			REVIEW FINDINGS			
IEP Objective	% Cor.	Date	Method	Materials	% Cor.	Notes
① What-do questions in drill a. What does it say? b. What does he/she do	80%	10-16-78	a. "See if I can read these words" b. "See if I know what these people"	Dolch Flash Cards PLDK Occupations	100% 0%	++++++ +6/6 000000 -6/6
② Plural -s marker in drill	90%	10-17-78	"Tell me what you see."	pictures of multiple copies of an object	88%	++0+++++ (ez= problem) +7/8
③ 2-dimensional display of prepositions	80%	10-10-78	"Tell me where the ___ is."	spatial relationship pictures	60% 100% 100% 50% 0%	on under in beside between
④ Act out S-V-O relationships in sentences	80%	10-10-78	"Make these dolls do what I tell you."	dollhouse figures & objects	86%	+++++0+ +6/7
⑤ Yes/No Questions in drill a. Can ___ b. Are ___ c. Is ___	90%	2-27-79	"You are going to find out how smart I am. Ask me if the ___"	a. Can ___ is → Fokes is doing cards b. are -s plural subject cards	100% 33% 100%	Can ++++++ +6/6 Are 0000++ +3/6 Is ++++++ +6/6
⑥ Past tense -ed marker in drill	80%	3-29-79	"Tell me what he did yesterday"	Fokes regular verb is doing cards	70%	++0++00+++ +7/10
⑦ Process semantics of he, she & they in sentences	90%	12-13-78	"Look at these people (man, women group) This is he, she, they. Point to the one I'm talking about"	flannel board figures	100%	He +4/4 She +4/4 They +4/4
⑧ Use infinitive to in drill	80%	1-25-79	"Tell what these people like to do"	pictures of singular subjects engaged in action	70%	+++0++++00 +7/10
⑨ Possessive -s in drill	86%	4-12-79	"This ___ belongs to ___. Tell me whose ___ this is."	3 figures who were given naming which demand -s;z-ez b. pictures of objects	100% 100% 0%	-s ++++ -z ++++ -ez 0000
⑩ Use of they in drill & sequential stories	100%	4-5-79	"Tell me what these people are doing"	Plural subject stimulus cards	100%	++++ +++ +7/7
⑪ Use of will in a story to show future tense	67%	5-10-79	"Tell me what this girl will do tonight"	DLM 127 sequential story of girl getting ready for bed	83%	+++++0+ +5/6
⑫ Receptively acknowledge difference between has/have	30%	5-10-79	"Tell me what he has and what they have."	Put 1 figure & a group down. place objects below each.	50% 50%	has ++0+0+00 4/8 have +0++00 3/6
⑬ Use of 3rd person singular in drill	20%	5-10-79	Before each response "Tell me what he does each day."	pictures of men engaged in actions	14%	0+00000 +1/7
⑭ Use of -ed to mark past tense in a sequential story	60%	5-10-79	"Tell me what happened yesterday"	DLM 127 sequential story	67%	0++ +2/3

APPENDIX 15
°Language Skills for a Compensatory Language Program*

A. Use of elaborated syntax:
   1. complex verb phrases
   2. complex noun phrases
   3. subordination
   4. infinitives

B. Use of a-precise language of reference:
   1. detailed description of parts of stimuli
   2. modifiers that are relational, explicit and coordinated
   3. pronouns with prior referents
   4. vocabulary that describes familiar objects and actions

C. Use of superordinate class names

D. Use of the following classes of words:
   1. uncommon adjectives
   2. uncommon adverbs
   3. logical connectives

E. Social:
   1. ability to get and maintain teacher's attention
   2. ability to ask questions of teacher

F. Ability to use information to give appropriate answers to questions

G. Reversal of conjoined words and phrases

H. Comprehension of contrasts between one's own speech and the standard dialect

°*nature of a language program for lower-class four-year-olds*

---

*From *Language Training in Early Childhood Education*, "Language Research and Preschool Language Training," Donald R. Moore (1971, p. 37).

APPENDIX 16
Bridging the Gaps in the Communication Process

What I think about, I can say.
What I can say, I can write.
What I can write, I can read.
I can read what I can write
and what other people have
written for me to read.
(Van Allen and Allen 1970, p. 21)

Language–Reading Experience

1. Have the child arrange sequential picture cards in the correct order so that they tell a story.

2. Have the child tell the story.

3. Type the story as the child tells it a second time. Ask questions about why the characters are doing some of the actions pictured, what is happening between frames of the story or what two actions are occurring simultaneously.

4. Let the child read aloud his story.

5. Discuss at that time or at the next session the various structural components used to make the story flow.

ONE DAY SUE AND JEN WANTED TO BAKE A CAKE, SO THEY DID. JEN HANDED HER THE CAKE MIX AND THEY STARTED TO MAKE THEIR CAKE. IN ORDER TO MAKE THEIR CAKE, THEY HAD TO ADD THREE EGGS AND THEN STIR THE BATTER. NEXT, SUE POURED THE BATTER INTO THE CAKE PANS, AND THEN SLIPPED THEM INTO THE OVEN TO BAKE. SHE SET THE TIMER BECAUSE SHE WANTED TO REMEMBER THE EXACT TIME THE CAKE WOULD BE BAKED. WHILE THE CAKE WAS BAKING, THEY WENT FOR A SWIM. THEY WERE RELAXING BY THE POOL, WHEN SUDDENLY THE TIMER RANG. SUE CAME IN AND TOOK THE CAKE OUT OF THE OVEN. THEY HAD A NICE SNACK OF CAKE AND MILK.

By L. Z.
3–15–77

REFERENCES

Adler, S. "Dialectal Differences: Professional and Clinical Implications," *Journal of Speech and Hearing Disorders* 36, 1 (1971), 90–100.

Aiken, L. R. "Language Factors in Learning Mathematics," *Review of Educational Research* 42 (1972), 359–85.

Arnold, K. S., and L. Reed. "The Grammatic Closure Subtest of the ITPA: A Comparative Study of Black and White Children," *Journal of Speech and Hearing Disorders* 41, 4 (1976), 477–485.

Ausberger, C. *Syntax One.* Tucson, Arizona: Communication Skill Builders, Inc. (1976).

Bates, E. "Pragmatics and Sociolinguistics in Child Language," in *Normal and Deficient Child Language,* D. M. Morehead and A. Morehead (eds.). Baltimore: University Park Press (1976), pp. 411–464.

Beilin, H. *Studies in the Cognitive Bases of Language Development.* New York: Academic Press (1975).

Bellugi–Klimi, U. "Some Language Comprehension Tests," in *Language Training in Early Childhood Education,* C. S. Lavetelli (ed.). Urbana, Illinois: University of Illinois Press (1971), pp. 157–169.

Bennett, C. L. "Language Intervention Systems for TMR: Action Programs in the Schools," American Speech and Hearing Convention, Las Vegas, Nevada (1974).

Bereiter, C., and S. Engelmann. *Teaching Disadvantaged Children in the Preschool.* Englewood Cliffs, New Jersey: Prentice–Hall (1966).

Berko, J. "Children's Learning of English Morphology," *Word* 14 (1960), 150–177.

Bernstein, B. "Social Class, Linguistic Codes and Grammatical Elements," *Language and Speech* 5 (1962), 221–240.

_____. "Elaborated and Restricted Codes: Their Social Origins and Some Consequences," *American Anthropologist* 66 (1964), 55–69.

_____. "A Socio–Linguistic Approach to Social Learning," in *Penguin Survey of the Social Sciences,* J. Gould (ed.). Baltimore: Penguin (1965), pp. 144–168.

_____. "Social Structure, Language and Learning," in *The Psychology of Language, Thought and Instruction,* J. P. de Cecco (ed.). New York: Holt, Rinehart and Winston (1967).

_____. "A Socio–Linguistic Approach to Socialization: With Some Reference to Educability" in *Language and Poverty,* F. Williams (ed.). Chicago: Markham Publishing Co. (1970), pp. 25–61.

Berry, M. D., and R. L. Erickson. "Speaking Rate: Effects on Children's Comprehension of Normal Speech," *Journal of Speech and Hearing Research* 16, 3 (1973), 367–374.

Biederman, S. "Integrating Language Exercises into Academic Curricula in a Self-Contained Language Disabilities Class," *Language, Speech and Hearing Services in Schools* 7, 1 (1976), 41–47.

Bloom, B. S. *Taxonomy of Educational Objectives, Handbook I: Cognitive Domain.* New York: David McKay Co., Inc. (1956).

Bloom, L. *Language Development: Form and Function in Emerging Grammars.* Cambridge: MIT Press (1970).

——————. "Language Development," in *Review of Child Development,* F. D. Horowitz (ed.). Chicago: University of Chicago Press (1975), Vol. 4, pp. 245–303.

Blue, C. M. "The Marginal Communicator," *Language, Speech and Hearing Services in Schools* 6, 1 (1975), 32–37.

Bonvillian, J. D., and K. E. Nelson. "Sign Language Acquisition in a Mute Autistic Boy," *Journal of Speech and Hearing Disorders* 41, 3 (1976), 339–347.

Bowerman, M. "Semantic and Syntactic Development," in *Bases of Language Intervention,* R. L. Schiefelbusch (ed.). Baltimore: University Park Press (1978), pp. 97–189.

Braine, M. D. S. "The Ontogeny of English Phrase Structure: The First Phase," *Language* 39 (1963), 1–13.

Bransford, J. D., and M. K. Johnson. "Contextual Pre-Requisites for Understanding: Some Investigations of Comprehension and Recall," *J. verb Learning. verb. Behav.* 11 (1972), 717–726.

Brookner, S. P., and N. O. Murphy. "The Use of a Total Communication Approach with a Non-Deaf Child: A Case Study," *Language, Speech and Hearing Services in Schools* 6, 3 (1975), 131–138.

Brown, R. "How Shall a Thing Be Called?" *Psychological Review* 65 (1958), 14–21.

——————. *A First Language.* Cambridge: Harvard University Press (1973).

Brown, R., and U. Bellugi. "Three Processes in the Child's Acquisition of Syntax," *Harvard Educational Review* 34 (1964), 133–151.

Burgemeister, B., L. Blum, and I. Lorge. *Columbia Mental Maturity Scale.* New York: Harcourt, Brace, Jovanovich (1972).

Burrows, E. H., and D. Neyland. "Reading Skills, Auditory Comprehension of Language and Academic Achievement," *Journal of Speech and Hearing Disorders* 43 (1978), 467–472.

Bush, C., and M. Bonachea. "Parental Involvement in Language Development: The PAL Project," *Language, Speech and Hearing Services in Schools* 4, 2 (1973), 82–85.

Carrow, E. *Test for Auditory Comprehension of Language.* Austin, Texas: Urban Research Group (1973).

——————. "A Test for Elicited Imitations in Assessing Grammatical Structure in Children," *Journal of Speech and Hearing Disorders* 39 (1974), 437–444.

Casey, L. "Development of Communication Behavior in Autistic Children by Use of Manual Signs," American Speech and Hearing Association Convention, Houston, Texas (1976).

Chappell, G. E., and G. A. Johnson. "Evaluation of Cognitive Behavior in the Young Nonverbal Child," *Language, Speech and Hearing Services in Schools* 7, 1 (1976), 17–27.

Chomsky, N. *Syntactic Structures.* The Hague: Mouton Press (1957).

Chon, R. "Arithmetic and Learning Disabilities," in *Progress in Learning Disabilities, Vol. 2,* H. R. Myklebust (ed.). New York: Grune and Stratton (1971), pp. 322–389.

Clay, M. M. "Reading Errors and Self-Correction Behavior," *British Journal of Educational Psychology* 38 (1969), 47–56.

Cronkhite, G., and K. Penner. "A Reconceptualization and Revised Scoring Procedure for the ITPA Based on Multivariate Analysis of the Original Normative Data," *Journal of Speech and Hearing Research* 18, 3 (1975), 506–520.

Dale, P. S. *Language Development: Structure and Function.* New York: Holt, Rinehart and Winston (1976).

De Renzi, E., and L. A. Vignolo. "The Token Test: A Sensitive Test to Detect Receptive Disturbances in Aphasics," *Brain* 85 (1962), 665–678.

de Villiers, P. A., and J. G. de Villiers. "On This, That and the Other: Non–Egocentricism in Very Young Children," *Journal of Experimental Child Psychology* 18 (1974), 438–447.

Dulay, H. C., and M. K. Burt. "Goofing: An Indicator of Children's Second Language Learning Strategies," *Language Learning* 22 (1973), 235–251.

Dulay, H. C., E. Hernandez–Chavez, and M. K. Burt. "The Process of Becomining Bilingual," in *Diagnostic Procedures in Speech, Hearing, and Language,* S. Singh and J. Lynch (eds.). Baltimore: University Park Press (1978), pp. 251–303.

Duncan, J., and R. D. Baskervill. "Responses of Black and White Children to the Grammatic Closure Subtest of the ITPA," *Learning, Speech and Hearing Services in Schools* 8, 2 (1977), 126–132.

Dunn, L. M. *Peabody Picture Vocabulary Test.* Circle Pines, Minnesota: American Guidance Service (1965).

Ervin–Tripp, S. "Sociolinguistics," an unpublished paper cited in Moore 1971 (later referenced) (1967).

_____. "Wait for Me, Roller–Skate," in *Child Discourse,* S. Ervin–Tripp and C. Mitchell–Kernan (eds.). New York: Academic Press (1977).

Fasold, R. W., and W. Wolfram. "Some Linguistic Features of Negro Dialect," *Learning, Speech and Hearing Services in Schools* 3, 4 (1972), 16–49.

Fristoe, Macalyne. *Language Intervention Systems for the Retarded.* Decatur, Alabama: Lurleen B. Wallace Development Center (1975).

Furth, H. G., and J. Youniss. "Formal Operations and Language: A Comparison of Deaf and Hearing Adolescents," in *Normal and Deficient Child Language,* D. E. Morehead and A. Morehead (eds.). Baltimore: University Park Press (1976), pp. 387–410.

Fygetakis and D. Ingram. "Language Rehabilitation and Programmed Conditioning: A Case Study," in *Papers and Reports on Child Language Development,* No. 4. Stanford, California: Stanford University Committee on Linguistics (1972), pp. 169–178.

Geller, E. F., and S. G. Wollner. "A Preliminary Investigation of the Communicative Competence of Three Linguistically Impaired Children," a paper presented at the New York Speech and Hearing Association (1976).

Gelman, R., and M. Shatz. "Appropriate Speech Adjustments: The Operation of Conversational Constraints on Talk of Two–Year–Olds," in *Interaction, Conversation and Development of Language,* M. Lewis and L. A. Rosenblum (eds.). New York: John Wiley and Sons (1977), pp. 27–61.

Gerber, A. *Goal: Carryover.* Philadelphia: Temple University Press (1973).

Gerber, A., E. B. Francis, and D. H. Ecroyd. "Nonstandard Negro English: A Rationale and Approach from One Urban University," a Short Course, American Speech and Hearing Association Convention, Detroit (1973).

Ginsburg, H. *Myth of the Deprived Child.* New Jersey: Prentice–Hall (1972).

Gleason, J. B. "Code–Switching in Children's Language," in *Cognitive Development and the Acquisition of Language,* T. E. Moore (ed.). New York: Academic Press (1973), pp. 159–167.

Glucksberg, S., and R. M. Krauss. "What Do People Say After They Have Learned to Talk? Studies of the Development of Referential Communication," *Merrill–Palmer Quarterly* 13 (1967), 309–316.

Glucksberg, S., R. M. Krauss, and R. Weisberg. "Referential Communication in Nursery School Children: Method and Some Preliminary Findings," *Journal of Exceptional Child Psychology* 3 (1966), 333–342.

Gordon, T. *Parent Effectiveness Training.* New York: Plume Books (1975).

Gray, B., and B. Ryan. *A Language Program for the Nonlanguage Child.* Champaign, Illinois: Research Press (1973).

Greenfield, P. M., and J. H. Smith. *Communication and the Beginnings of Language: The Development of Syntactic Structures in One Word Speech and Beyond.* New York: Academic Press (1976).

Grice, H. P. "Logic and Conversation," in *Syntax and Semantics, Vol. 3: Speech Acts,* P. Cole and H. L. Morgan (eds.). New York: Academic Press (1975).

Guilford, J. P. *The Nature of Human Intelligence.* New York: McGraw–Hill (1967).

Halliday, M. A. K. *Explorations in the Functions of Language.* London: Edward Arnold Publishers, Ltd. (1973).

——————— *Learning How To Mean: Explorations in the Development of Language.* London: Edward Arnold Publishers, Ltd. (1975).

——————— *Language As Social Semiotic.* Baltimore: University Park Press (1978).

Hammer–Eden, E. F. "A Comparison of the Oral Language Patterns of Mature and Immature First Grade Children." Doctoral dissertation, Arizona State University, Tempe, Arizona (1969).

Hannah, E. P. *Applied Linguistic Analysis, II.* Pacific Palisades, California: SenCom Associates (1977).

Heider, E. "Style and Effectiveness of Children's Verbal Communications Within and Between Social Classes." Doctoral dissertation, Harvard University (1968).

Holland, A. L. "Language Therapy for Children: Some Thoughts on Context and Content," *Journal of Speech and Hearing Disorders* 30, 4 (1975), 514–523.

Hymes, D. "Competence and Performance in Linguistic Theory," in *Language Acquisition: Models and Methods,* R. Huxley and E. Ingram (eds.). New York: Academic Press (1971), pp. 3–24.

Ingram, D. "The Acquisition of the English Verbal Auxiliary and Copula in Normal and Linguistically Deviant Children," in *Papers and Reports on Child Development,* No. 14. Stanford, California: Stanford University Committee on Linguistics (1972).

Katz, J. J., and D. T. Langedoen. "Pragmatics and Presuppositions," *Language* 52 (1976).

Kavanagh, J. F. (ed.). *Communicating by Language: The Reading Process.* Bethesda, Maryland: National Institute of Child Health and Human Development (1968).

Kirk, S. A., J. J. McCarthy, and W. D. Kirk. *The Illinois Test of Psycholinguistic Abilities* (rev. ed.). Urbana, Illinois: University of Illinois Press (1968).

Kirk, S. A., and W. D. Kirk. "Uses and Abuses of the ITPA," *Journal of Speech and Hearing Disorders* 43, 1 (1978), 58–75.

Kleffner, R. R. "Hearing Losses, Hearing Aids and Children with Language Disorders," *Journal of Speech and Hearing Disorders* 38, 2 (1973), 230–239.

Krauss, R. M., and G. S. Rotter. "Communication Abilities of Children as a Function of Status and Age," *Merrill-Palmer Quarterly* 14 (1968), 160–173.

Kresheck, J. D., and L. Nicolosi. "A Comparison of Black and White Children's Scores on the PPVT," *Language, Speech and Hearing Services in Schools* 4, 1 (1973), 37–40.

Labov, W. "The Logic of Non-Standard English," in *Language and Poverty*, F. Williams (ed.). Chicago: Markham Publishing Company (1970), pp. 153–189.

Labov, W., and P. Cohen. "Systematic Relations of Standard and Nonstandard Rules in the Grammars of Negro Speakers," *Project Literary Reports* 8 (1966), 66–84.

Lasky, E. Z., and A. M. Chapandy. "Factors Affecting Language Comprehension," *Language, Speech and Hearing Services in Schools* 7, 3 (1976), 159–168.

Lawton, D. "Social Class Language Differences in Group Discussions," *Language and Speech* 7 (1964), 183–204.

Lee, L. L. *Northwestern Syntax Screening Test*. Evanston, Illinois: Northwestern University Press (1969).

_____. "A Screening Test for Syntax Development," *Journal of Speech and Hearing Disorders* 35 (1970), 103–112.

Lee, L. L., R. A. Koenigsknecht, and S. T. Mulhern. *Interactive Language Development Teaching*. Evanston, Illinois: Northwestern University Press (1974).

Leonard, L. B. "What is Deviant Language?" *Journal of Speech and Hearing Disorders* 37 (1972), 427–446.

Leonard, L. B., C. Prutting, J. A. Perozzi, and R. K. Berkley. "Nonstandardized Approaches to the Assessment of Language Behaviors," *Asha*, 20, 5 (1978), 371–379.

Levin, H., and E. L. Kaplan. "Listening, Reading and Grammatical Structure," in *Perception of Learning*, D. L. Horton and J. J. Perkins (eds.). Columbus, Ohio: Charles E. Merrill Publishing Co. (1971), pp. 1–16.

Lipman, M., A. M. Sharp, and F. S. Oscanyan. *Philosophy in the Classroom*. Upper Montclair, New Jersey: Institute for the Advancement of Philosophy for Children (1974).

Loban, W. *Language Ability in the Middle-Grades of Elementary School*. U.S. Office of Education (1961).

_____. *The Language of Elementary School Children*. National Council of Teachers of English Research Report, No. 1. Champagne, Illinois: National Council of Teachers of English (1963).

_____. *Language Development: K–12*. Urbana, Illinois: National Council of Teachers of English (1976).

Longhurst, T. M., and T. A. M. Schrandt. "Linguistic Analysis of Children's Speech: A Comparison of Four Procedures," *Journal of Speech and Hearing Disorders* 38 (1973), 240–249.

Longhurst, T. M., and S. Grubb. "A Comparison of Language Samples Collected in Four Situations," *Language, Speech and Hearing Services in Schools* 5, 2 (1974), 71–78.

Luria, A. R. *Higher Cortical Functions in Man*. New York: Basic Books (1966).

Mattingly, I. G. "Reading, the Linguistic Process and Linguistic Awareness," in *Language by Ear and by Eye*, J. F. Kavanagh and I. G. Mattingly (eds.). Cambridge: MIT Press (1972), pp. 133–147.

Mayberry, R. "If a Chimp Can Learn Sign Language, Surely My Nonverbal Client Can Too," *Asha* 18, 4 (1976), 223–228.

MacDonald, E. *Articulation Testing and Treatment: A Sensory–Motor Approach*. Pittsburgh: Stanwix House (1964).

MacDonald, J. D. *Environmental Language Inventory* (ELI). Columbus, Ohio: Charles E. Merrill Publishing Company (1978).

MacDonald, J. D., and J. P. Blott. "Environmental Language Intervention: The Rationale for a Diagnosis and Training Strategy Through Rules, Context and Generalization," *Journal of Speech and Hearing Disorders* 39, 3 (1974), 244–256.

McNeil, M. R., and T. E. Prescott. *Revised Token Test*. Baltimore, Maryland: University Park Press (1978).

McNeill, D. *The Acquisition of Language: The Study of Developmental Psycholinguistics*. New York: Harper and Row (1970).

Monroe, M. "Necessary Preschool Experiences for Comprehending Reading," *Reading and Inquiry*, International Reading Association Conference Proceedings, Vol. 10. Newark, Delaware: International Reading Association (1965).

Monsees, E. K., and C. Berman. "Speech and Language Screening in a Summer Headstart Program," *Journal of Speech and Hearing Disorders* 33 (1968), 121–126.

Moore, D. R., "Language Research and Preschool Language Training," in *Language Training in Early Childhood Education*, C. S. Lavetelli (ed.). Urbana, Illinois: University of Illinois Press (1971), pp. 3–47.

Morehead, D. M., and M. Johnson. "Piaget's Theory of Intelligence Applied to the Assessment and Treatment of Linguistically Deviant Children," in *Papers and Reports on Child Language Development*, No. 4. Stanford, California: Stanford University Committee on Linguistics (1972), pp. 143–162.

Mowrer, D. "An Analysis of Motivational Techniques," *Asha* 12 (1970), 10.

Muma, J. "Language Intervention: Ten Techniques," *Language, Speech and Hearing Services in Schools* 5 (introductory issues) (1971), 7–17.

_____. "Language Assessment: Some Underlying Assumptions," *Asha* 15, 7 (1973), 331–338.

Nelson, K. *Structure and Strategy in Learning to Talk*. Monograph of the Society for Research in Child Development, No. 149 (1973).

Nelson–Burgess, S. A. "Mira: A Concept in Receptive Language Assessment of Bilingual Children," *Language, Speech and Hearing Services in Schools* 6, 1 (1975), 24–28.

Nicolosi, L., and J. D. Kresheck. "Variability in Test Scores on Form A and Form B of the PPVT," *Language, Speech and Hearing Services in Schools* 3, 1 (1972), 44–45.

O'Brien, C. *The Language Different Child*. Columbus, Ohio: Charles E. Merrill Publishing Co. (1973).

Olswang, L. B., and R. L. Carpenter. "Elicitor Effects on the Language Obtained from Young Language–Impaired Children," *Journal of Speech and Hearing Disorders* 43, 1 (1978), 76–88.

Osser, H. "Developmental Studies of Communicative Competence," in *Sociolinguistics: A Crossdisciplinary Perspective.* Washington, D.C.: Center for Applied Linguistics (1969).

Panagos, J. M. "Persistence of the Open Syllable Reinterpreted as a Symptom of Language Disorders, *Journal of Speech and Hearing Disorders* 39, 1 (1974), 23-31.

Piaget, J. *The Language and Thought of the Child.* Translated by M. Gabain. Cleveland: Meridian Press (1955).

Pollack, E., and N. Rees. "Disorders of Articulation — Some Clinical Applications of Distinctive Feature Theory," *Journal of Speech and Hearing Disorders* 37 (1972), 451-461.

Prutting, C. A., T. M. Gallagher, and A. Mulac. "The Expression Portion of the NSST Compared to a Spontaneous Language Sample," *Journal of Speech and Hearing Disorders* 40 (1975), 40-48.

Ratusnik, D. L., and R. A. Koenigsknecht. "Cross-Cultural Item Analysis of the Columbia Mental Maturity Scale: Potential Application by the Language Clinician," *Language, Speech and Hearing Services in Schools* 7, 3 (1976), 186-189.

Reddell, R. B., "The Effect of Oral and Written Patterns of Language Structure on Reading Comprehension," *Reading Teacher* 18 (1965), 270-275.

Rees, N. S. "Pragmatics of Language," in *Bases of Language Intervention,* R. L. Shiefelbusch (ed.). Baltimore: University Park Press (1978), pp. 193-268.

Rees, N. S., and M. Shulman. "I Don't Understand What You Mean by Comprehension," *Journal of Speech and Hearing Disorders* 43, 2 (1978), 208-219.

Rosenthal, W. S., J. Eisenson, and J. M. Luchau. "A Statistical Test of the Validity of Diagnostic Categories Used in Childhood Language Disorders: Implications for Assessment Procedures," in *Papers and Reports on Child Language Development,* No. 4. Stanford, California: Stanford University Committee on Linguistics (1972), pp. 121-141.

Ryan, R. "Point-Counterpoint: Are Speech Pathology and Audiology Sciences or Art?" an informal debate, American Speech and Hearing Convention, San Francisco, California (1978).

Schiller, A., and W. A. Jenkins. *In Other Words.* Glenview, Illinois: Scotts Foresman and Company (1977).

Schlesinger, I. M. "Production of Utterances and Language Acquisition," in *The Ontogenesis of Language,* D. T. Slobin (ed.). New York: Academic Press (1971).

Searle, J. R. *Speech Acts.* London: Cambridge University Press (1969).

Shatz, M., and R. Gelman. " The Development of Communication Skills: Modification in the Speech of Young Children as a Function of the Listener," *Monograph of the Society for Research on Child Development* 38, 5 (1973), 1-37.

Siegel, G. M., and P. A. Broen. "Language Assessment," in *Communication Assessment and Intervention Strategies,* L. L. Lloyd (ed.). Baltimore: University Park Press (1976), pp. 73-122.

Sigel, I. E., and R. R. Cocking. *Cognitive Development from Childhood to Adolescence.* New York: Holt, Rinehart and Winston (1977).

Simon, C. S. "Talk Time: Language Development in Readiness Classes," *Language, Speech and Hearing Services in Schools* 6 (1975), 161-168.

_____. "Environmental Language Inventory: A Laudatory Comment," *Journal of Speech and Hearing Disorders* 41, 4 (1976), 557-558.

_____. "Cooperative Communication Programming: A Partnership Between the Learning Disabilities Teacher and the Speech–Language Pathologist," *Language, Speech and Hearing Services in Schools* 8 (1977), 188–200.

_____. "Language Expansion with Culturally Different Children: An Explanation and Guide for Primary Teachers," *Kentucky English Bulletin* Fall 1977.

_____. "The Use of Language Teaching Methodologies to Improve Reading Related Skills," in *Remediation of Language Disorders,* J. R. Andrews and M. S. Burns (eds.). Evanston, Illinois: Institute for Continuing Professional Education (1978).

_____. "Philosophy for Learning Disabled Students," *Thinking: A Journal of Child Philosophy* 1 (1979), 21–34.

Skelley, M., L. Schinsky, R. W. Smith, and R. S. Fust. "American Indian Sign (Amerind) as a Facilitator for Verbalization for the Oral Verbal Apraxic," *Journal of Speech and Hearing Disorders* 39, 4 (1974), 445–456.

Skinner, B. F. *Verbal Behavior.* New York: Appleton–Century–Crofts (1957).

Slobin, D. I. "Imitation and Grammatical Development in Children," in *Contemporary Issues in Developmental Psychology,* N. S. Endler, L. R. Boulter and H. Osser (eds.). New York: Holt, Rinehart and Winston (1968), pp. 437–443.

Steiner, G. "The Language Animal," *Encounter* 33 (1969), 7–24.

Streng, A. H. *Syntax, Speech and Hearing.* New York: Grune and Stratton (1972).

Strickland, R. G. *Language of Elementary School Children: Its Relationship to the Language of Reading Textbooks and to the Quality of Reading of Selected Children,* Bulletin of the School of Education, Indiana University. Bloomington, Indiana: School of Education (Indiana University) (1962).

Sullivan, E. T., L. W. Clark, and E. W. Tiegs. *California Test of Mental Maturity.* Monterey, California: California Test Bureau (1961).

Swisher, L. "Treatment and Evaluation of the Language of the Autistic Child," Mini-seminar, American Speech and Hearing Association Convention, Washington, D.C. (1975).

Tyack, D., and R. Gottsleban. *Language Sampling, Analysis and Training.* Palo Alto, California: Consulting Psychologists Press (1974).

Van Allen, R., and C. Allen. *An Introduction to Language Experiences in Reading: Level I* (Teacher's Resource Book). Encyclopedia Britannica Press (1970).

Vogel, S. A. *Syntactic Abilities in Normal and Dyslexic Children.* Baltimore: University Park Press (1976).

Weiss, M., and M. Duffy. "Syntactic Slot–Filler: An Alternative to Davis' Sentence Construction Board," *Journal of Speech and Hearing Disorders* 39, 2 (1974) 230–231.

Wiig, E. H., and E. M. Semel. *Language Disabilities in Children and Adolescents.* Columbus, Ohio: Charles E. Merrill Publishing Company (1976).

Williams, F. (ed.). *Language and Poverty.* Chicago: Markham Publishing Company (1970).

Williams, R., and W. Wolfram. *Social Dialects: Differences vs. Disorders,* a monograph of the American Speech and Hearing Association. Rockville, Maryland: ASHA (1977).

Yudkovitz, E., and J. Rottersman. "Language Therapy in Childhood Schizophrenia: A Case Study of a Monitoring and Feedback Approach," *Journal of Speech and Hearing Disorders* 38, 4 (1973), 520–532.

INDEX

A language remediation materials set so complete you could name a course after it

Communicative Competence: A Functional-Pragmatic Language Program
by Charlann S. Simon (1980)

Here's a different kind of language program that can bring your dream of the "most efficient use of your time" closer to reality. In one package are all the diagnostic and therapeutic tools needed to help you speed individual progress to each student in your caseload.

These materials are theoretically based, literature referenced, practical and *highly* accessible to the student, instructor and practicing professional.

The author has blended the work of Muma, Bloom, Schlesinger, Ingram, Morehead (and many others) with a decade of constant trial and refinement of ideas from her own clinical practice. The result is a current yet readable synthesis of thought and practice in language remediation.

With the aid of these new materials, students of all ages can learn how to formulate effective messages that are listener oriented, coherent, fluent and composed of adult grammar.

The scope of this umbrella program extends from basic two-word utterances to complex sentences and presents methods for developing cognitive skills—reason, logic and assessment of values.

The materials of the kit include 644 racially-balanced stimulus cards that reflect ideas, feelings and activities of interest to school children. Rather than segregated by part of speech they are categorized by specific semantic-grammatical rules; elaborations of these basic constructions; and categories of objects and people. They include:

Agent Action (male)
Agent Action (female)
Action Object (male)
Action Object (female)
Agent Action (group)
Action Object (group)
Negation (rejection)
Negation (denial)
Negation (nonexistence)
Dative
Object/Location
People/Location
Possessive Pronoun (male)
Possessive Pronoun (female)
Possessive Pronoun (group)
Plurals
Possession
Comparative
Reflexive Pronouns
Structural Prepositions
Combining Ideas
Modals (will)
Modals (could, might, would)
Modals (should, can)
Modifying Words (nouns and adjectives)
Modifying Phrases
Transportation
Careers
Household Objects
Animals
Chores
Storytelling

Communicative Competence is an important teaching aid that belongs with your most useful clinical tools

Games
Problem-Solving Situations
Illustrative Verb
Embedding
Verb Analysis
Logic
Science Experiments
Fables/Proverbs

The **Communicative Competence** Complete Program shows you how to keep current with new research. It helps you discover ways to employ that research in your clinical practice and to shift emphasis from syntax drill to true communication therapy.

The conceptual model enables you to determine each student's difficulties with message sending, then helps you choose the corrective strategy to implement.

The depth and flexibility of the program allows the clinician to use the materials effectively with a wide range of students (PK-12). The program includes all of the following lightweight and easily portable components:

1. **The Monograph**—147-page framework for developing an operational model of competent-vs.-incompetent communication skills, gathering a language sample, analyzing data and formulating IEP goals and short-term objectives.

2. **The Teaching Manual**—360-page *Suggested Strategies for a Functional-Pragmatic Approach to Language Therapy* presenting hundreds of clinical tasks that can be programmed with the program's stimulus materials. Sample IEP's are provided for each clinical task.

3. **Filmstrips**—Four full-color filmstrips (249 frames) containing 25 real-life sequential situations, modifying words and modifying phrases. Also included is a portable non-electric, hand-held filmstrip viewer.

4. **Photo-Diagram Book**—96-page full-color printed reproductions of the filmstrip sequences. You'll be able to follow a student's descriptions as he or she views the filmstrips, or work with the student without filmstrips. Also includes color photos for modifying words and phrases and specific labeling. A black-and-white section has diagrams and explanations of appliances, vehicles and sports.

5. **Stimulus Cards**—473 full-color photos plus 171 black-and-white illustrations on 4" x 6" cards depicting situations the child must describe accurately. Tabbed index dividers included for ease in locating specific cards.

6. **Spinners**—14 different 8½" x 8½" spinner boards offering various stimuli.

All materials are easily accessible in a durable storage box.

Developmental Age: 6–17

Major Objectives: The client will develop non-egocentric communication skills; the client will establish rudimentary and refined syntactic and pragmatic skills so as to send a structurally correct, coherent message composed of sufficient information to a listener; the professional will develop an operational model of competent-vs.-incompetent communication skills.

Applicable: Language Development.

Communicative Competence: A Functional-Pragmatic Language Program (Complete)
#2510-3 .... **$250**
147-page monograph, 8½" x 11", softbound; 360-page teaching manual, 8½" x 11", spiral wire bound; 96-page photo-diagram book, 11" x 8½", spiral wire bound; 4 filmstrips plus viewer; 644 stimulus cards, 4" x 6", plus tabbed index dividers; 14 spinner boards, 8½" x 8½", plastic laminated; storage box (total weight, 12 pounds).

Communication Skill Builders, Inc.
3130 N. Dodge Blvd./P.O. Box 42050
Tucson, Arizona 85733
(602) 327-6021